Academic Encounters

2nd Edition

Miriam Espeseth
Series Editor: Bernard Seal

4

LISTENING

SPEAKING

CAMBRIDGE
UNIVERSITY PRESS

CAMBRIDGE
UNIVERSITY PRESS

32 Avenue of the Americas, New York, NY 10013-2473, USA

Cambridge University Press is part of the University of Cambridge.

It furthers the University's mission by disseminating knowledge in the pursuit of education, learning and research at the highest international levels of excellence.

www.cambridge.org
Information on this title: www.cambridge.org/9781107603011

First published 1999
Second edition 2012
3rd printing 2013

Printed in the United States of America

A catalog record for this publication is available from the British Library.

ISBN 978-1-107-60298-4 Student's Book with DVD
ISBN 978-1-107-60302-8 Class Audio CDs
ISBN 978-1-107-60301-1 Teacher's Manual

Additional resources for this publication at www.cambridge.org/academicencounters

Art direction, book design, and photo research: Integra
Layout services: Integra
Audio production: John Marshall Media
Video production: Steadman Productions

Table of Contents

Scope and Sequence

Unit 1: Mind, Body, and Health • 1

	Content	Ⓛ Listening Skills	Ⓢ Speaking Skills
Chapter 1 **The Influence of Mind over Body** page 3	**Interview 1** The Stress of Teaching First-Graders **Interview 2** The Stress of Being a Police Officer **Lecture** Stress and the Immune System	Following directions Listening for specific information Listening for tone of voice Drawing inferences	Predicting the content Personalizing the topic Comparing information from different sources Asking for opinions Sharing your cultural perspective
Chapter 2 **Lifestyle and Health** page 20	**Interview 1** Starting Smoking and Trying to Quit **Interview 2** Quitting Smoking and How It Changes Your Life **Lecture** Risk Factors in Cardiovascular Disease	Following directions Anticipating answers Drawing inferences	Recalling what you already know Predicting the content Combining information from different sources Asking for confirmation Sharing your cultural perspective

Unit 2: Development Through Life • 45

	Content	Ⓛ Listening Skills	Ⓢ Speaking Skills
Chapter 3 **The Teen Years** page 47	**Interview 1** Being a Teenager in a Different Culture **Interview 2** Starting a New Life in One's Teens **Lecture** Erik Erikson's Fifth Stage of Psychosocial Development: Adolescence	Recording numbers Listening for specific information Completing multiple-choice items Uses of *like* in casual speech Correcting or expressing a negative politely	Examining graphics Using background information to make predictions Reviewing predictions Summarizing what you have heard Combining information from different sources Sharing your cultural perspective
Chapter 4 **Adulthood** page 65	**Survey** The Best Age to Be **Lecture** Developmental Tasks of Early Adulthood	Recording numbers Summarizing what you have heard Uses of *get* Listening for specific information	Predicting the content Responding to true/false statements Identifying who said what Sharing your personal perspective Eliciting a conclusion Applying general concepts to specific data Sharing your personal and cultural perspective

V Vocabulary Skills	N Note Taking Skills	Learning Outcomes
Reading and thinking about the topic Examining vocabulary in context Building background knowledge on the topic Breaking down words to guess their meaning Guessing vocabulary from context Learning words as they are used	Summarizing data Using telegraphic language Summarizing what you have heard	Prepare and deliver an oral presentation on health and healthy habits
Reading and thinking about the topic Examining vocabulary in context Building background knowledge on the topic Guessing vocabulary from context	Paraphrasing what you have heard Using symbols and abbreviations Outlining practice	

V Vocabulary Skills	N Note Taking Skills	Learning Outcomes
Reading and thinking about the topic Examining vocabulary in context Building background knowledge on the topic Guessing vocabulary from context Considering different perspectives	Using space to show organizational structure Organizational structure	Prepare and deliver an oral presentation on a particular period of life
Reading and thinking about the topic Examining vocabulary in context Building background knowledge on the topic Guessing vocabulary from context	Creating a chart Paying attention to signal words	

Unit 3: Nonverbal Messages • 85

	Content	**L** Listening Skills	**S** Speaking Skills
Chapter 5 Body Language page 87	**Interview 1** Brazilian Body Language **Interview 2** Korean Body Language **Interview 3** Japanese Body Language **Lecture** Body Language Across Cultures	Reading nonverbal cues Responding to true/false statements Determining which way *this* or *that* is pointing Using your body to communicate	Recalling what you already know Thinking critically about the topic Considering related information Looking beyond the facts Sharing your personal and cultural perspective
Chapter 6 Touch, Space, and Culture page 102	**Interview 1** Marcos: Touch and Space **Interview 2** SunRan: Touch and Space **Interview 3** Airi: Touch **Lecture** Nonverbal Communication: The Hidden Dimension of Communication	Summarizing what you have heard Decoding the meaning of word stress Listening for stress and intonation	Recalling what you already know Personalizing the topic Sharing your cultural perspective Considering related information Using comparison/contrast Analyzing cultural content Sharing your personal and cultural perspective

Unit 4: Interpersonal Relationships • 125

	Content	**L** Listening Skills	**S** Speaking Skills
Chapter 7 Friendship page 127	**Interview** Friendships **Lecture** Looking at Friendship	Listening for specific information Retelling Listening for verb tense and aspect	Personalizing the topic Drawing inferences Sharing your personal and cultural perspective Forming generalizations Sharing your personal perspective Considering related information
Chapter 8 Love page 143	**Interview** Courtship and Making Marriage Work **Lecture** Love: What's It All About?	Listening for details Listening for specific information Listening for digressions Showing interest	Personalizing the topic Sharing your cultural perspective Sharing your personal and cultural perspective Considering related information Conducting an interview Applying general concepts to specific data

V Vocabulary Skills	N Note Taking Skills	Learning Outcomes
Reading and thinking about the topic Examining vocabulary in context Guessing vocabulary from context	Restating what you have heard Mapping	Prepare and deliver an oral presentation comparing body language in two cultures
Reading and thinking about the topic Examining vocabulary in context Guessing vocabulary from context Comparing information from different sources	Recording information Reading nonverbal cues Recalling what you already know Summarizing what you have heard	

V Vocabulary Skills	N Note Taking Skills	Learning Outcomes
Reading and thinking about the topic Examining vocabulary in context Describing a typical scene and activities Reminiscing about a typical scene and activities Building background knowledge on the topic: Culture notes Building background knowledge on the topic: Statistics on friendship Guessing vocabulary from context	Recalling what you already know Summarizing what you have heard Using morphology, context, and nonverbal cues to guess meaning	Prepare and deliver an oral presentation on a famous friendship or love relationship
Reading and thinking about the topic Examining vocabulary in context Building background knowledge on the topic Guessing vocabulary from context	Conducting a survey using the Likert scale Taking advantage of rhetorical questions Outlining Practice	

Introduction

The *Academic Encounters* Series

Academic Encounters is a sustained content-based series for English language learners preparing to study college-level subject matter in English. The goal of the series is to expose students to the types of texts and tasks that they will encounter in their academic course work and provide them with the skills to be successful when that encounter occurs.

At each level in the series, there are two thematically paired books. One is an academic reading and writing skills book, in which students encounter readings that are based on authentic academic texts. In this book, students are given the skills to understand texts and respond to them in writing. The reading and writing book is paired with an academic listening and speaking skills book, in which students encounter discussion and lecture material specially prepared by experts in their field. In this book, students learn how to take notes from a lecture, participate in discussions, and prepare short presentations.

The books at each level may be used as stand-alone reading and writing books or listening and speaking books. Or they may be used together to create a complete four-skills course. This is made possible because the content of each book at each level is very closely related. Each unit and chapter, for example, has the same title and deals with similar content, so that teachers can easily focus on different skills, but the same content, as they toggle from one book to the other. Additionally, if the books are taught together, when students are presented with the culminating unit writing or speaking assignment, they will have a rich and varied supply of reading and lecture material to draw on.

A sustained content-based approach

The *Academic Encounters* series adopts a sustained content-based approach, which means that at each level in the series students study subject matter from one or two related academic content areas. There are two major advantages gained by students who study with materials that adopt this approach.

- Because all the subject matter in each book is related to a particular academic discipline, concepts and language tend to recur. This has a major facilitating effect. As students progress through the course, what at first seemed challenging feels more and more accessible. Students thus gain confidence and begin to feel that academic study in English is not as overwhelming a task as they might at first have thought.

- The second major advantage in studying in a sustained content-based approach is that students actually gain some in-depth knowledge of a particular subject area. In other content-based series, in which units go from one academic discipline to another, students' knowledge of any one subject area is inevitably superficial. However, after studying a level of *Academic Encounters* students may feel that they have sufficiently good grounding in the subject area that they may decide to move on to study the academic subject area in a mainstream class, perhaps fulfilling one of their general education requirements.

The four levels in the series

The *Academic Encounters* series consists of four pairs of books designed for four levels of student proficiency. Each pair of books focuses on one or more related academic subject areas commonly taught in college-level courses.

- *Academic Encounters* 1: The Natural World
  Level 1 in the series focuses on earth science and biology. The books are designed for students at the low-intermediate level.

- *Academic Encounters* 2: American Studies
  Level 2 in the series focuses on American history, politics, government, and culture. The books are designed for students at the intermediate level.
- *Academic Encounters* 3: Life in Society
  Level 3 in the series focuses on sociological topics. The books are designed for students at the high-intermediate level.
- *Academic Encounters* 4: Human Behavior
  Level 4 in the series focuses on psychology and human communication. The books are designed for students at the low-advanced to advanced level.

New in the Second Edition

The second edition of the *Academic Encounters* series retains the major hallmark of the series: the sustained content approach with closely related pairs of books at each level. However, lessons learned over the years in which *Academic Encounters* has been on the market have been heeded in the publication of this brand new edition. As a result, the second edition marks many notable improvements that will make the series even more attractive to the teacher who wants to fully prepare his or her students to undertake academic studies in English.

New in the series

Four units, eight chapters per level. The number of units and chapters in each level has been reduced from five units / ten chapters in the first edition to four units / eight chapters in the second edition. This reduction in source material will enable instructors to more easily cover the material in each book.

Increased scaffolding. While the amount of reading and listening material that students have to engage with has been reduced, there has been an increase in the number of tasks that help students access the source material, including a greater number of tasks that focus on the linguistic features of the source material.

Academic Vocabulary. In both the reading and writing and the listening and speaking books, there are tasks that now draw students' attention to the academic vocabulary that is embedded in the readings and lectures, including a focus on the Academic Word list (AWL). All the AWL words encountered during the readings and lectures are also listed in an appendix at the back of each book.

Full color new design. A number of features have been added to the design, not only to make the series more attractive, but more importantly to make the material easier to navigate. Each task is coded so that teachers and students can see at a glance what skill is being developed. In addition, the end-of-unit writing skill and speaking skill sections are set off in colored pages that make them easy to find.

New in the reading and writing books

More writing skill development. In the first edition of *Academic Encounters*, the reading and writing books focused primarily on reading skills. In the second edition, the two skills are much more evenly weighted, making these books truly reading and writing books.

End-of-chapter and unit writing assignments. At the end of each chapter and unit, students are taught about aspects of academic writing and given writing assignments. Step-by step scaffolding is provided in these sections to ensure that students draw on the content, skills, and language they studied in the unit; and can successfully complete the assignments.

New and updated readings. Because many of the readings in the series are drawn from actual discipline-specific academic textbooks, recent editions of those textbooks have been used to update and replace readings.

New in the listening and speaking books

More speaking skill development. In the first edition of *Academic Encounters*, the listening and speaking books focused primarily on listening skills. In the second edition, the two skills in each of the books are more evenly weighted.

End-of-unit assignments. Each unit concludes with a review of the academic vocabulary introduced in the unit, a topic review designed to elicit the new vocabulary, and an oral presentation related to the unit topics, which includes step-by-step guidelines in researching, preparing, and giving different types of oral presentations.

New and updated lectures and interviews. Because the material presented in the interviews and lectures often deals with current issues, some material has been updated or replaced to keep it interesting and relevant for today's students.

Video of the lectures. In addition to audio CDs that contain all the listening material in the listening and speaking books, the series now contains video material showing the lectures being delivered. These lectures are on DVD and are packaged in the back of the Student Books.

The *Academic Encounters* Listening and Speaking Books

Skills

The *Academic Encounters* listening and speaking books have two main goals. The first is to help students develop the listening and note taking skills needed to succeed in academic lecture settings. The second goal is to help students build confidence in their speaking ability – in casual conversation, classroom discussion, and formal oral presentations.

To this end, tasks in the *Academic Encounters* listening and speaking books are color-coded and labeled as L **L** Listening Skill tasks, V **V** Vocabulary Skill tasks, S **S** Speaking Skill tasks, and N **N** Note Taking Skill tasks. At the beginning of each unit, all the skills taught in the unit are listed in a chart for easy reference.

- **Listening Skills L.** The listening skill tasks are designed to promote success in a variety of listening contexts, from brief instructions to extended academic lectures, and for a wide range of purposes including listening for specific details, identifying general ideas, and evaluating extra-linguistic features such as tone of voice.

- **Vocabulary Skills V.** Vocabulary learning is an essential part of improving one's ability to understand spoken language, especially in an academic setting. It is also key to oral expression. Pre-listening vocabulary tasks throughout the book provide context for interviews and lectures. Exercises stress the importance of guessing from context. Oral activities also include suggested words and expressions. Each end-of-unit review features both a written and oral academic vocabulary review activity to reinforce the academic words that have been introduced.

- **Speaking Skills S.** The speaking skills exercises in the book are designed to introduce and facilitate the practice of language and communication skills that students will need to feel comfortable in casual social contexts as well as academic settings. They range from presenting personal opinions to conducting an interview. Language models are provided.

- **Note Taking Skills N.** Lecture note taking is key to academic success, and is thus a major focus of the *Academic Encounters* listening and speaking books. In each chapter, the lecture section introduces a specific aspect of note taking, providing a focus for listening to the lecture itself and for follow-up comprehension checks. Additional non-academic note taking skills are practiced throughout each chapter and frequently "recycled" for maximum practice.

The audio program

Authentic listening material, based on real interviews and lectures, forms the basis of the chapter material. Each chapter includes a warm-up listening exercise to introduce the topic, informal interviews that explore different aspects of the topic, and a two-part academic lecture on related material. These different types of listening expose students to varied styles of discourse, and they all recycle the chapter's concepts and vocabulary.

The complete audio program is available on audio CDs. In addition, a DVD containing the lecture delivered by a lecturer in front of a classroom is included in the back of the *Student Book*. Transcripts of the lectures are also provided in the back of the *Student Book* and the complete transcript of all this listening material is included in this *Teacher's Manual*.

Tasks

Whenever a task type occurs for the first time in the book, it is introduced in a colored commentary box that explains what skill is being practiced and why it is important. At the back of the book, there is an alphabetized index of all the skills covered in the tasks.

Order of units

The units do not have to be taught in the order in which they appear, although this is generally recommended since tasks increase in complexity, and because note taking tasks may draw on skills originally presented in an earlier chapter. However, teachers who wish to use the material in a different order may consult the scope and sequence in the front of the *Student Book* or the Skills Index at the back of the *Student Book* to see the information that has been presented in earlier units.

Course length

Each chapter in the *Academic Encounters* listening and speaking books represents approximately 10 hours of classroom material. The new end-of-unit activities may take an additional 3 hours of class time. Multiple opportunities exist to lengthen the course by the addition of related material, longer oral presentations, movies, debates, and guest speakers on the chapter topics. However, the course may also be made shorter. Teachers might choose not to do every task in the book and to assign some tasks as homework, rather than do them in class.

Quizzes

The *Academic Encounters* series adopts a sustained content-based approach in which students experience what it is like to study an academic discipline in an English-medium instruction environment. In such classes, students are held accountable for learning the content of the course by the administering of tests.

In the *Academic Encounters* series, we also believe that students should go back and study the content of the book and prepare for a test. This review of the material in the books simulates the college learning experience, and makes students review the language and content that they have studied.

At the back of this *Teacher's Manual* are eight reproducible lecture quizzes containing short-answer questions. Students should complete these quizzes after they listen to the lecture and do all related exercises.

General Teaching Guidelines

In this section, we give some very general instructions for teaching the following elements that occur in each unit of the *Academic Encounters* listening and speaking books:

- The unit opener, which contains a preview of the unit content, skills, and learning outcomes
- The *Getting Started* sections, which help students prepare for the chapter topic
- The *Real-Life Voices*, which are short interviews with people of all ages and backgrounds on the chapter topic the chapter topic
- The *In Your Own Voice* sections, which provide students with an opportunity to discuss their own opinions on the topic
- The *Lectures*, which are at the end of each chapter
- The *Unit Review* activities, which include vocabulary reviews and an oral presentation. These are included at the end of each unit

Unit Opener

The opening page of the unit contains the title of the unit, a photograph related to the content of the unit, and a brief paragraph that summarizes the unit. Have the students discuss what the title means. Have them look at the art on the page, describe it, and talk about how it might relate to the title. Read the paragraph summarizing the unit contents as a class, making sure that students understand the vocabulary and key concepts. At this point it is not necessary to introduce the unit topics in any depth.

The second page lists the unit contents: the titles of the two chapters within the unit and the titles of the interviews and lecture in each of the two chapters. Have students read the titles and check for understanding.

After reviewing the contents, have students focus on the listening, speaking, vocabulary, and note taking skills that they will be practicing in the unit. Ask students if they recognize any of the skills listed. It is not necessary for them to understand all of the terms used at this point, since the skills will be introduced and explained when they appear in the unit. Finally, go over the *Learning Outcomes*. Explain to students that the subject matter and the language skills that they will be learning throughout the unit will help them prepare for this final oral presentation.

The unit opener section should take less than an hour of class time.

Getting Started

This section contains material that is designed to activate students' prior knowledge about the topic, provide them with general concepts or vocabulary, and stimulate their interest. The section begins with a photograph, cartoon, or image. Have students look at the image and read the questions about it. Here and throughout, maximize opportunities for students to develop oral fluency and confidence by having them answer and discuss in pairs or small groups before reviewing as a class.

A short reading related to the chapter topic follows. Have students read and then respond orally to the comprehension and discussion questions that follow. The questions are designed to go beyond the reading and elicit language and concepts that will be presented in the chapter, so encourage students to volunteer their own information and ideas.

An introductory listening activity concludes this section. The type of listening task is determined by the chapter content. It may involve completing a chart, doing a matching exercise, or listening for specific information. The task provides skill-building practice and also gives students listening warm-up on the chapter topic. Make sure that students understand what is expected of them before they listen, and replay as needed so that all students feel successful. The follow-up comprehension and discussion questions can be answered as a class, in pairs, or in small groups.

The *Getting Started* section should take about one hour of class time.

Real-Life Voices

Real-Life Voices, which contains one or more informal interviews on topics related to the chapter content, is divided into three sub-sections:

Before the Interview(s)

This sub-section contains a pre-listening task that calls on students either to predict the content of the interview or to share what they already know about the topic from their personal or cultural experience. Be sure to take enough time with this task for all students to contribute. Students can also benefit here from each other's background knowledge.

Interview(s)

Because unfamiliar vocabulary is a great stumbling block to comprehension, each listening activity is preceded by a glossed list of terms (many of them colloquial) that will be heard in the interview. Have students review the vocabulary.

The next task prepares students to understand the content of the interview excerpt that they will hear; a variety of task types are used, including true-false statements, incomplete summaries, and short-answer questions. Have students review this task carefully as it will help them focus on the pertinent information as they listen to the interview excerpt.

After they have listened to all of the interview(s) and checked their comprehension, an additional listening exercise directs the students' attention to a specific aspect of language use featured in the interview(s), such as verb tense or tone of voice.

After the interview(s)

This sub-section provides students with activities to demonstrate and deepen their understanding of the concepts presented in the interviews. It may involve synthesizing information from a short reading or drawing inferences about material in the interviews. Encourage all students to contribute their opinions.

The *Real-Life Voices* section should take three to four hours of class time.

In Your Own Voice

This section builds on the content presented up to this point in the chapter and also focuses on one or more language functions (for example, asking for opinions, expressing interest, expressing polite negatives) that either were used in the *Real-Life Voices* interviews or are relevant to discussion of the chapter topics. Semi-structured speaking activities elicit the functional language, relate to the chapter content, and encourage students to share their own information. Language examples are given. Allow students to practice the language with a number of partners, and perform for the class if they like. The focus is on developing confidence with the functional language required for casual conversation and discussion.

The *In Your Own Voice* section should take approximately one hour of class time.

Academic Listening and Note Taking

This section, which is constructed around a recording of an authentic academic lecture, is divided into three sub-sections:

Before the Lecture

This sub-section begins with a brief introduction of the lecture topic and the person who is giving the lecture. Read it as a class and ask students about any language that is unfamiliar. Encourage students to guess at the meaning of unfamiliar words.

The following task either provides background information on the lecture or elicits what students may already know about the lecture topic. Topics in the book are chosen to be of general interest, so encourage that interest in students by asking them to volunteer what they already know. Some students will likely have studied the lecture material in their first language; let them become the experts in providing context for their classmates.

Finally, this sub-section introduces a specific academic note taking skill that is determined by the language of the lecture itself and sequenced to build on skills studied in previous chapters. A language box explains the skill in detail. Go over this explanation as a class and answer any questions. The sub-section concludes with a short listening activity featuring lecture excerpts that focus on the specific note taking skill.

Lecture

Each lecture is divided into two parts, for ease of comprehension. Before they listen, students complete a vocabulary exercise that focuses on the academic vocabulary in the lecture that is likely to be unfamiliar. The vocabulary is presented in the context in which students will hear it; encourage them to guess at the meaning.

Following the vocabulary task, students preview a comprehension task designed to provide a framework for their listening and note taking. The task may involve completing a summary or outline, or answering comprehension questions. Then, students listen to the lecture itself, practicing the note taking skills they have learned. Make it clear to students that for most of the lecture comprehension tasks, their answers need not be word-for-word the same. Encourage them to paraphrase.

After the Lecture

This sub-section invites students to share their perspective through discussion questions that allow them to analyze the chapter content more critically, often by comparing it to new written or graphic material. Students may be asked to apply what they have learned to their own situations. As with other discussion activities included throughout the chapter, this activity will help students prepare for the final oral presentation in two ways: they will develop oral skills and confidence, and they will identify what aspects of the unit content they are most interested in exploring further.

The *Academic Listening and Note Taking* section should take about four or five hours.

Unit Review

This section includes a review of academic vocabulary and unit topics, and culminates in an oral presentation:

Academic Vocabulary Review

The *Academic Vocabulary Review* can be done in class or as homework. As with all vocabulary activities in the book, it stresses the importance of context. As you review the vocabulary words, ask students to recall the context in which they learned them. If a word has been used to mean different things in different chapters (for example, "depressed"), elicit that information as well.

A second vocabulary review activity asks students to answer questions about the unit content; relevant vocabulary words are provided. This activity may be done orally in pairs or small groups. Students may then volunteer sentences to be written on the board, providing a class review of the unit.

Oral Presentation

Each of the unit reviews concludes with a different type of oral presentation. Carefully scaffolded activities, presented in three steps, encourage students to work on oral delivery:

- *Before the Presentation*
- *During the Presentation*
- *After the Presentation*

Before they make their presentations, students are generally instructed to choose or define a topic they will discuss. They may be asked to present to a small or large group, individually or in a team. The organization of the presentation depends on the parameters established in each chapter, but students may be asked to research their topic online or study language related to introducing or structuring a topic. Instructors should monitor the students' choice of topic and make sure they understand how best to structure their allotted time.

The *During the Presentation* section instructs students about speaking clearly, taking time to define new words, using appropriate body language, and other mechanisms for making effective presentations. This is the students' chance to work on their oral delivery and make sure that the audience understands their presentation. This is the instructor's chance to work on oral delivery skills.

After the presentation, students learn to check that their listeners have understood their presentation. They learn language to check for comprehension, engage in self-assessment, and learn how to respond to others' presentations with questions and comments.

The *Unit Review* should take three to four hours of class time, depending on the number of students in the class and the time that instructors decide to dedicate to this activity.

Chapter 1
The Influence of Mind over Body

1 Getting Started

1 Reading and thinking about the topic Pages 3–4
B

1. major: loved one's death, divorce; minor: waiting in line, getting stuck in traffic jams
2. Stress affects the immune system.
3. learn to handle and relieve stress

2 Following directions Page 4
B

1. crying baby; thunder and rain; ocean waves on the shore; children laughing loudly; a cat purring; a jet taking off; police sirens
2.–4. *Answers will vary.*

2 Real-Life Voices

Interview 1 – The stress of teaching first-graders

1 Personalizing the topic Page 6
B

Students should have checked the following signs:
Great fatigue
Increased feelings of anger when small things go wrong
Frequent colds and infections

2 Listening for specific information Page 6
A

1. for 20 years; 3-year-olds, preschool, and elementary school
2. Children bring problems to class; one disruptive child can disturb the entire class; a teacher cannot forget about work when she goes home.
3. She has to be very patient all day with her class.
4. She works very closely with the children, and they often have colds or flu; teaching is stressful, and stress can lower one's resistance to illness.
5. She exercises regularly and talks to her friends.

Interview 2 – The stress of being a police officer

2 Listening for specific information Page 8
B

1. for 25 years
2. Patrol is the most stressful assignment because of the fear factor. A patrol officer never knows how people will react to being stopped.
3. Police officers have more everyday illnesses, ulcers, and heart disease than the average adult.
4. exercise programs, psychological counseling, and discussion groups
5. He's a baseball fan, he gets daily exercise, and he has a good relationship with his wife.

3 Listening for tone of voice Page 8
A

1. b   2. a   3. a   4. b

After the Interviews

1 Comparing information from different sources Pages 8–9
B

Nancy: Become part of a support system; take care of your health.

Sam or the
LAPD: Become part of a support system; take care of your health; make time for yourself. Note: It may also be inferred that the LAPD teaches patrol officers to anticipate stressful situations (the routine traffic stop).

2 Drawing inferences Page 9
A

Answers may vary. The most likely answers are:
1. D   2. A   3. A   4. A   5. A
6. D   7. A

4 Academic Listening and Note Taking

Before the Lecture

1 Building background knowledge on the topic Pages 12–13
B

Answers may vary. Suggested answers:

Psycho- = related to the mind
Somatic- = related to the body

D

Food (an unconditioned stimulus) naturally makes a dog salivate (an unconditioned response). If we always ring a bell (a conditioned stimulus) as we feed the dog, after a while the dog will salivate even without the food (a conditioned response).

2 Using telegraphic language Page 13
B

research* shows: imm. syst. Hurt by stress (*animal & hum.) – 2
headache, high bld. press. etc – more docs now treat w/relax. techniques (not drugs) – 4
headache, heart dis, high bld. press. etc (health probs) – may be part psych. – 1
med. profs: mind affects body – esp. neg. if feel 'helpless, no control'. – 3

Lecture Part 1 – Psychoneuroimmunology (PNI) and Animal Studies on Stress

1 Breaking down words to guess their meaning Page 14
A

psych- is related to the mind or thinking. (4)
-logy, -logic, or -logical describes the study of a subject. (3)
pre- refers to something happening before. (1)
mal- usually refers to something bad. (2)
phys- has something to do with the body. (5)

2 Guessing vocabulary from context Pages 14–15
B

1. b   2. d   3. h   4. c   5. g
6. i   7. a   8. e   9. f

C

1. b   2. b   3. c   4. b   5. c   6. c

3 Summarizing what you have heard Pages 15–16
C

Wording will vary; alternatives are shown in brackets.

There is a lot of evidence to support the idea that our minds can affect our bodies. Many of the health problems that people suffer, such as headaches, high blood pressure, and heart disease [skin rashes, high cholesterol], may be related to psychosomatic disorders – that is, they may be caused by the mind. The field of psychoneuroimmunology (PNI) studies the way in which our minds can affect our immune systems. In a healthy person, the immune system protects the body against disease [illness]. Animal and human research has shown that stress – especially uncontrollable stress – can hurt the immune system. Robert Ader did an important study with rats in which he learned, quite by accident, that the rats' immune systems could be conditioned to malfunction [not work correctly]. This was an exciting discovery for science: if the immune system can be taught to not work correctly [malfunction], that probably means that it can also learn to heal itself.

Lecture Part 2 – Human Research on PNI

1 Learning words as they are used Page 17
A

1. c   2. a   3. a   4. b   5. c   6. b

2 Guessing vocabulary from context Pages 17–18
A

Answers may vary. Suggested completions:

1. taxes
2. older people, elderly people
3. usually, generally
4. meditation, yoga, breathing; Aspirin

3 Summarizing what you have heard Page 18

c

Wording will vary; some alternatives are shown in brackets.

There are also <u>human</u> studies to support the idea that the mind can <u>influence the body</u> [<u>affect the body</u>]. Simply thinking about stressful situations can <u>depress</u> the immune system. This has been seen in studies on accountants before tax time, and on <u>students</u> before <u>exams</u>. Also, if people feel out of <u>control</u> in their lives, this can compromise their <u>immune systems</u>. Studies show that people in nursing homes who didn't choose to <u>live there</u> are more likely to get sick than people who <u>did</u>. People in the <u>medical</u> [<u>health care</u>] field are becoming more interested in PNI. We see this, for example, in the treatment of headaches and <u>sleeplessness</u> [<u>high blood pressure</u>]; more doctors and nurses today are teaching their <u>patients</u> to control these problems not with medication, but rather with <u>relaxation techniques</u>.

Chapter 2
Lifestyle and Health

1 Getting Started

1 Reading and thinking about the topic Page 21
B

1. prevent heart disease
2. The graphic does not mention controlling weight or going to the doctor.
3. No; it uses the phrase "prevent heart disease," which means to avoid getting heart disease.

2 Recalling what you already know Page 22

Answers will vary. Suggested answers:

1. how fast the heart beats
2. Put your finger on your wrist or neck and count the beats.
3. Blood is pushed through the heart.
4. It gets faster when we are using our muscles and when we feel excited or afraid.

3 Following directions Page 23
B

Answers will vary. Suggested answers:

1. Yes, because the heart was pumping extra blood to the muscles. Blood carries oxygen, and the muscles needed extra oxygen to do the extra work.
2. Possible answers: When we are in a stressful situation, when we are afraid, or when we are doing something fun and exciting, the heart rate increases.
3. In general, a slow heart rate indicates a healthier heart.

2 Real-Life Voices

Interview 1 – Starting smoking and trying to quit

2 Anticipating answers Page 25
B

1. 13; 14
2. 20; 5
3. cool
4. pack and a half

5. will power
6. heart attack; hospital
7. No
8. energy; breathing; biking; running; easier; stopped smoking
9. heart attack; wouldn't

Interview 2 Part 1 – Quitting smoking

2 Paraphrasing what you have heard Page 27
B

Wording will vary; alternatives are shown in brackets.

How She Started — Donna started smoking at about age <u>16</u> or <u>17</u>. She and her friends would get together after <u>school</u>. They would eat <u>candy</u> and smoke cigarettes. Donna's <u>parents</u> didn't know about it.

Addicted to Cigarettes — After a while, Donna was smoking a <u>pack</u> a day. She kept smoking for <u>13</u> more years. Donna studied in South <u>America</u> and later she taught in <u>Mexico</u>. In both places, smoking was more <u>common</u> than in the United States. People smoked in public places – for example, in <u>movie theaters</u>, <u>buses</u>, and <u>supermarkets</u> [<u>classrooms</u>, <u>taxicabs</u>].

Trying to Quit — But Donna wasn't feeling very <u>well</u>. She had chronic bronchitis. She tried to <u>quit</u> smoking many times but could not. Later, when she was married and <u>pregnant</u>, she almost completely stopped smoking. But it was very <u>painful</u> for her, and as soon as her <u>son</u> was born, she started <u>smoking</u> again.

Interview 2 Part 2 – How quitting smoking changes your life

2 Paraphrasing what you have heard Page 29
B

Students may use synonyms (e.g., children rather than kids); the words shown are from the audio script.

Social Pressure — Donna's friends and even her <u>sister</u> really pressured her to stop smoking especially when she was around their <u>kids</u>.

Hypnotherapy — Finally, a friend of Donna's recommended a hypnotherapist. This friend had been a very heavy smoker – <u>3</u> packs a <u>day</u> – but the hypnotherapist had helped him <u>quit</u> and the treatment was painless. Donna decided to go and try it herself, and the treatment worked! Donna believes that she was successful this time for two reasons: (1) Hypnotherapy was the right method for her; and (2) she was finally fed up with smoking and ready to quit.

Donna's Son and Smoking — Donna does not think that her son will ever start smoking because he hated it when she smoked. He worried about her health. However, if he *did* start smoking, she would do everything she could to educate him about the health dangers of smoking before he became addicted to cigarettes.

The Benefits of Quitting — As soon as she quit smoking, Donna started to feel better physically; she had more energy, and she could smell things again. Also, food started to taste better to her. She started exercising to control her weight. A final advantage was saving money.

3 Drawing inferences Page 30
A

1. c   2. b   3. a   4. b

After the Interviews
Combining information from different sources Pages 30–31
A

Answers designated as ? (inferences) will vary.

		Pat	Donna
Why did you start smoking?	Peer pressure	x	x
	It was "cool."	x	x
	Cigarette advertising	?	?
What physical problems did smoking cause?	Heart disease	x	
	Bronchitis	?	x
	Low energy	?	?
	Inability to taste and smell	?	?
What method(s) did you use to try to quit?	Will power	x	x
	Candy		x
	Hypnosis		x
Do you ever feel like smoking now?	Yes		
	No	x	x
What advice would you give to people trying to quit smoking?	Talk to them about the health dangers		x
	No advice	x	
In what ways is your life better now?	Enjoy taste of food more	x	x
	More physically active	x	x
	Easier to breathe	x	x
	More energy	x	x
	Save money		x
What physical activities do you enjoy?	Backpacking	?	
	Biking	?	?
	Running	?	

4 Academic Listening and Note Taking

Before the Lecture

1 Building background knowledge on the topic Page 34

B

1. referring to the blood vessels
2. An artery carries blood *from* the heart; a vein carries blood *to* the heart.
3. tubular

3 Using symbols and abbreviations Pages 35–36

A

1. m	2. l	3. j	4. k	5. e
6. d	7. o	8. f	9. a	10. c
11. h	12. i	13. n	14. b	15. g

D

Wording and abbreviations will vary:

1. CVD = ♥ attack, stroke, PVD
2. ♂ risk for CVD (♀ risk)
3. Obese = ≥ 20% over ideal wt. = risk diabetes, HBP
4. Stress MAY → HBP & cholest., smoking, eating → CVD.

Lecture Part 1 – Unalterable Risk Factors in CVD

1 Guessing vocabulary from context Page 37

B

1. g	2. a	3. k	4. j	5. h	6. b
7. e	8. i	9. c	10. d	11. f	

2 Outlining practice Page 38

C

Wording and abbreviations will vary:

I. CVD = heart attack, stroke, peripheral vascular disease
   A. ♥ attack = part. or complete block'g of artery to ♥ muscle
   B. Stroke = block'g of ≥1 arteries to brain
   C. PVD = peripheral vascular disease – "clots to legs"

II. Unalterable risk factors
   A. Gender: <50, ♀ protected by estrogen: risk for CVD less than ♂
   B. Age: older = risk for CVD
   C. Diabetes = risk for CVD – reason not known.
   D. Family history: usually too high cholesterol – can be hereditary.

Lecture Part 2 – Alterable Risk Factors in CVD

1 Guessing vocabulary from context Pages 38–39

B

1. h	2. b	3. d	4. g
5. a	6. e	7. c	8. f

2 Outlining practice Page 39

C

Wording and abbreviations will vary.

III. Alterable risk factors
   A. HBP – Controlled w/ medicat'n – few side effects
   B. Obesity (≥20% over ideal wt.) may → diabetes and HBP
   C. Cigarette smok'g → CVD
   D. Psychosoc. (= soc. isolat'n, pers., daily stress – e.g. work) may → BP, cholest., smoking, overeating → CVD
   E. Sedentary lifestyle (= no exercise) → risk for CVD

Unit 1 Academic Vocabulary Review

1 Word forms Pages 40–41

1. analysis; analyzed
2. depressive; depress
3. environment; environmental
4. medications; medical; medicine
5. relevance; relevant
6. unpredictable; predict; unpredictability; Predictable
7. complexity
8. isolated; isolation
9. occurs; occurrence
10. Statistics; statistically

Chapter 3
The Teen Years

1 Getting Started

3 Recording numbers Page 49
A

The following information should be recorded on the graph:

James at age:
10: 4'10"
14: 5'1"
16: 5'8"
18: 5'11"
21: 6'
22: 6'1"

Sarah at age:
10: 4'9"
12: 5'4"
15: 5'8"
18: 5'9"

Interview 1 – Being a teenager in a different culture

2 Listening for specific information Pages 52–53
B

Word choices may vary.

1. 18
2. Iran; girls
3. freedom; understood
4. mother; father; driver's license; return; Iran; happy
5. friends; mother
6. with their parents; get married
7. 19; alone [by himself]; money; hard [bad, difficult]; good [helpful]; self-confidence
8. brother; 3; older; Iran; nice
9. dentist; Iran

Interview 2 – Starting a new life in one's teens

2 Completing multiple-choice items Pages 53–54
B

1. d   2. b   3. c   4. d
5. d   6. b   7. d   8. b

3 Uses of *like* in casual speech Pages 54–55
A

1. for example
2. as if
3. verb to like
4. verb to like
5. wait, I'm thinking
6. as if
7. wait, I'm thinking
8. similar to
9. wait, I'm thinking
10. hedge

4 Academic Listening and Note Taking

Before the Lecture

1 Building background knowledge on the topic Pages 57–58
A

Wording may vary.

1. through our interactions with other people [social interactions]
2. become competent in a specific area of life
3. If a person does not achieve competence at a particular stage, he feels inadequate.

2 Using space to show organizational structure Pages 58–59
A

Drugs/alcohol, other mind-altering substances
  Pressure to make decisions abt. use
  Much research
    Kids who use dr./alc. stop psychol./emotional growth
    Drug = protective screen betw. adolesc. and reality
    Chronic use → devel. stops
"Instant information"
  Internet, Ipods, Iphones
    Issue since TV invented: how affect develop. brain? we don't know
    Comput./video games – diff. from TV: "hypnotizing"

Lecture Part 1 – Adolescence: Identity vs. Role Confusion

1 Guessing vocabulary from context Pages 60–61

B

1. i	2. b	3. l	4. n	5. e
6. a	7. m	8. f	9. c	10. g
11. h	12. o	13. k	14. j	15. d

2 Organizational structure Page 61

C

Notes will vary.

(adolesc = age abt. 12–16)
Primary work = establ. own ID
    If unable? → "role confus."
        = cannot make good choices, know what
            yr. choices are
Components of adolesc work
    Challenge: phys & genital matur.
        -Confusing for kids because bodies chnge v. fast
        -Rapid phys. growth e.g., 6 in. (15.24 cm) in 2 mos.
        Result: adolesc very very self-absorbd.

Same time: social pressure from self and others
    to "grow up"
        = establish ego ID,
            think beyond own phys. feelgs,
            keep basic trust: "I cn make it thru this"
            Big challenge – many kids have probs.
            ("hit the wall")
Material challenge = choose career
    Many kids postpone: get educ.
    BUT – most adolescs feel anxiety about job choice
Falling in love → gender ID
    Very import. aspect at this period
    Related to ego ID because adolesc faces new
        aspects of self
    Dramatic change – can be wonderful or not - but
        always v. challeng'g

Lecture Part 2 – Identity vs. Role Confusion: New Challenges

1 Guessing vocabulary from context Pages 62–63

B

1. c	2. o	3. k	4. m	5. d
6. b	7. l	8. i	9. g	10. j
11. a	12. n	13. e	14. h	15. f

Chapter 4
Adulthood

1 Getting Started

1 Reading and thinking about the topic Pages 65–66

B

1. young adulthood, middle adulthood, and late adulthood
2. Young adulthood is the time for many important decisions. In middle adulthood, we face physical changes and changes in our family. In late adulthood, we continue to change physically. Our children have left home, and people in our age group begin to get sick and die, but we have more free time.

3 Recording numbers Page 66

A

Name	Age Now	Best Age
Bruce	28	Late 20s
Julie	25	4-9
Ann	57	30s
David	45	His age now
Otis	70	25-30 years
Gene	71	He doesn't know
Laurie	68	her age now; 40s
Loleta	77	from college graduate to marriage

2 Real-Life Voices

Survey Part 1 – The Best Age to Be

2 Responding to true/false statements Page 68

B

1. T   2. F   3. T   4. F   5. T
6. T   7. T   8. T   9. F

Survey Part 2 – The Best Age to Be

2 Summarizing what you have heard Page 69

B

Wording will vary. Alternatives are given in brackets.

Otis is a retired university professor. He says that his best teaching years were between <u>35</u> and <u>50</u> because he was more open to new ideas, <u>he lectured better,</u> and <u>he read a lot more.</u> At the age of <u>50,</u> he created <u>four new courses.</u> However, Otis feels that in another sense, his last <u>10</u> years have been the best <u>because he has become more mature [more responsible and sensitive to the world around him].</u>

Laurie and Gene are married. They are both painters. Laurie remembers her <u>40s</u> as a great time because she got her master's degree, <u>she had more time to paint,</u> and <u>she started studying music.</u>

Gene says that the older he gets, <u>the more he thinks about his youth.</u> Especially when he wakes up in the morning, he notices that <u>he doesn't feel so well [his bones and his joints hurt].</u> He and Laurie talk about how long <u>it takes them to get going in the morning.</u> When he was a young man, in the Army, he used to <u>get up and be ready in 10 minutes.</u> But now <u>it takes a long time.</u>

3 Uses of *get* Pages 69–70

A

1. over   5. older
2. ----   6. up
3. out of   7. going
4. used to

B

1. b   2. a   3. c   4. g   5. d   6. f   7. e

4 Academic Listening and Note Taking

Before the Lecture

2 Paying attention to signal words Pages 74–75

A

1. b   2. c   3. b   4. e   5. d   6. a   7. f

C

Wording and abbreviations will vary.

1. life chgs need to make as grow up
2. finan., emot., soc,
3. as = (adults)
4. adult kids live w/par.
5. diffic. estab. finan. indepen.
6. crisis pt. in fam. when child goes
7. 2 imp. tasks yng adult hd

Lecture Part 1 – Separation from Parents

1 Guessing vocabulary from context Page 75
B

1. e	2. h	3. f	4. i	5. a
6. d	7. c	8. j	9. g	10. b

2 Listening for specific information Page 76
C

Notes and abbreviations will vary.

Developmental Tasks of Young Adulthood (Pt. 1)
Young adulthood = from early or mid-20s
   in Western culture, young adult should be financially, emot., & soc. indep. from parents.
1st task = separate from parents & create new rel'ship based on mut. adulthd.
   – process really began early childhd.
   Financial indep: happening later in U.S. today because of econ.
   indep: not always successful: child keeps chld role, parent …
   – crisis time because change (many pple afraid)

Lecture Part 2 – The Crisis of Intimacy vs. Isolation

1 Guessing vocabulary from context Pages 76–77
B

1. e	2. j	3. h	4. b	5. g	6. i	7. d
8. f	9. m	10. l	11. c	12. a	13. k	

2 Listening for specific information Page 78
B

Wording and abbreviations will vary.

Developmental Tasks of Young Adulthood (Pt . 2)
2nd task - traditionally leads to marriage
   *called "crisis of intim. vs isol."
   If child develops hlthy ego identity as adolesc, → able to join w/other (marry) in young adulthd.
   – person must be able to compromise, sacrfc., negot.
   – if successful → intim, connect.
   – if not succ. → isolation
      – others see you as self-absorbd, e.g. – scientist who works all the time, never sees fam.
      – isolation is not natural; person is afraid to be hurt.
      – Success w/intimacy depends on devel. hlthy ID in adolesc.
Marriage in the West today: staying single longer
   – have freedom to take risks, move to new place
   – skepticism abt. marr bec. divorce rate
   → wait until ≥ late 20s → much lower divorce rt.
If young adults succeed at 2 tasks → fut. success & life satisf.

Unit 2 Academic Vocabulary Review

1 Word forms Page 80

1. establishment; to establish
2. theorized; theory
3. challenge(s); challenging
4. adapt; Adaptability
5. achieve; achievement
6. commitment; commit

Chapter 5
Body Language

1 Getting Started

2 Reading nonverbal cues Page 88

B

a. 7   b. 5   c. 2   d. 1
e. 4   f. 3   g. 6   h. 8

2 Real-Life Voices

Interview 1 – Brazilian body language

2 Responding to true/false statements Page 90
B

1. F   2. T   3. T   4. T   5. T   6. F

Interview 2 – South Korean body language

2 Responding to true/false statements Page 91
B

1. F   2. T   3. F   4. F   5. T   6. F

Interview 3 – Japanese body language

2 Restating what you have heard Pages 92–93
B

Word choice will vary. Some alternatives are given in brackets.

Airi is married to <u>an American</u>, and she has lived in the United States for <u>9 months</u>. Airi discovered one difference in body language between Americans and <u>Japanese</u> when she saw herself in a <u>family picture</u> [<u>formal portrait</u>] taken at her <u>husband's sister's</u> [<u>sister-in-law's</u>] wedding. All of the people in the picture were <u>smiling</u> with their <u>teeth</u> showing – except for <u>Airi</u> [<u>her</u>]. She felt <u>embarrassed</u> when she saw the picture.

Airi thinks that Japanese and Americans have similar attitudes about eye contact: In both countries, it's good for people to <u>look at each other</u> [<u>make eye contact</u>] when they're talking because it shows that they <u>are really listening</u> [<u>are really trying to understand</u>].

Airi has noticed that Americans use more <u>gestures</u> [<u>hand signals</u>] than Japanese. However, Airi says that she is more like an American in this respect: She started using a lot of <u>gestures</u> when she met <u>her husband</u> because it was so difficult to <u>communicate</u>.

3 Determining which way this or that is pointing Page 93
A

1. →   2. ←   3. ← OR →   4. ←   5. ←

B

Wording may vary.

1. it's very important for North Americans to have eye contact
2. you were trying to focus
3. a difference between Brazilians and Americans OR A part of my family was from Italy…
4. your wife is North American
5. opening and closing your hand

4 Academic Listening and Note Taking

Before the Lecture

2 Mapping Page 98
B

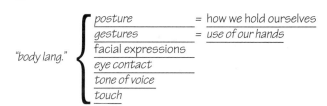

"body lang." {
posture = how we hold ourselves
gestures = use of our hands
facial expressions
eye contact
tone of voice
touch

Lecture Part 1 – Aspects of Body Language

1 Guessing vocabulary from context Page 99
A

1. c   2. b   3. a   4. a   5. b   6. b   7. a

2 Mapping Page 99
B

Wording and abbreviations may vary.

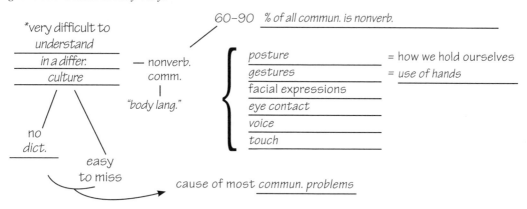

Lecture Part 2 – Cross-Cultural Misunderstandings

1 Guessing vocabulary from context Page 100
A

1. b   2. c   3. b   4. a   5. b   6. a

2 Mapping Page 100
B

Wording and abbreviations may vary.

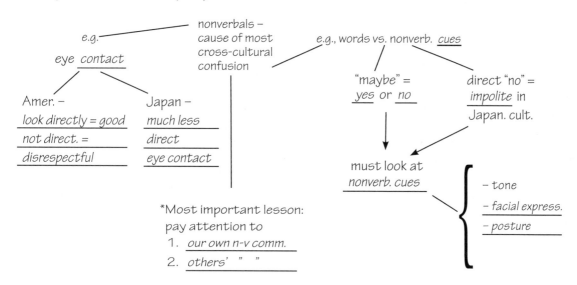

Chapter 6
Touch, Space, and Culture

1 Getting Started

2 Recording information Pages 103–104
B

zone	feet/inches	meters/cms
Public	>12 ft	>3.6 m
Business/social	6 ft	1.8 m
Personal	1 ft 6 in	46 cm
Intimate	<18 in	<50 cm

C

North America (NA): 46 cm
Western Europe (WE): 36–41 cm
Japan (J): 91 cm
Middle East (ME): 20–30 cm

2 Real-Life Voices

Interview 1 – Marcos: touch and space

2 Summarizing what you have heard Page 106
B

Word choice will vary. Some alternatives are given in brackets.

Marcos remembers an experience when he was talking to a <u>student</u> of his from <u>South Korea</u>. After a while, he noticed that the student had <u>backed up</u> into a <u>corner</u> because Marcos kept moving <u>closer to him</u> [toward him]. The student obviously felt very <u>uncomfortable</u>. Marcos had <u>invaded</u> his <u>body bubble</u> [space, personal space]. Marcos tries to stand <u>farther away</u> from people now that he lives in the United States so that they won't feel <u>uneasy</u> [uncomfortable, threatened]. Marcos also finds that he and his <u>wife</u> touch one another <u>less in public</u> in the United States than they did in <u>Brazil</u>.

Interview 2 – SunRan: touch and space

2 Summarizing what you have heard Page 107
A

Word choice will vary. Some alternatives are given in brackets.

SunRan learned to <u>shake hands</u> when she came to the United States, but she has to remember <u>not to do that</u> [not to shake hands] when she visits <u>South Korea</u>. She says that it is not good for <u>men</u> and <u>women</u> to <u>touch each other</u> in public in her country, but people of the same <u>sex</u> can hold <u>hands</u>. However, SunRan has to remember not to do that in the <u>US</u>.

When she first came to the United States, SunRan was <u>shocked</u> [very surprised] by the fact that <u>kids</u> [high school kids] hug and <u>kiss</u> at school.

SunRan noticed some changes in <u>South Korean</u> body language last time she visited her country. For example, <u>people shake hands more now</u>, and young couples <u>touch</u> [hold hands].

Interview 3 – Airi: touch

2 Summarizing what you have heard Page 108
A

Word choice will vary. Some alternatives are given in brackets.

Airi says that most Japanese people <u>never</u> hug and kiss one another. Her American husband felt <u>confused</u> by this at first: He thought his wife's family didn't <u>love him</u>. When Airi and her <u>husband</u> moved to the United States, she was <u>really confused</u> [uncomfortable] at first because her American family <u>always hugged and kissed</u> [would hug and kiss]. But now she <u>really likes it</u> [feels comfortable with it, enjoys it].

Recently, Airi visited Japan. When she met an old friend, she <u>opened her arms to give her a hug</u> [tried to hug her]. The friend looked <u>shocked</u> [afraid].

3 Decoding the meaning of word stress Page 109

A

1. touch: changing the subject
2. male friends: this (not that)
3. never: strong feeling
4. you: changing the subject
5. child: this (not that)
6. now: this (not that)
7. shocked: strong feeling

C

2. that = males & females
5. that = adult
6. that = before I came to the US

4 Academic Listening and Note Taking

Before the Lecture

2 Listening for stress and intonation Pages 114–115

B

Key - underlined for high or rising, *italics* for falling, **bold** for stress

1. How much of those expressions are conveyed through **verbal** communication? More often than not, our intense emotions are conveyed **non**verbally.
2. More often than not, our intense emotions are conveyed **non**verbally through gestures, body position, facial expression, vocal cues, eye contact, use of space, and *touching*.
3. Imagine what would happen if you don't understand this bubble. What might you experience? Possibly discomfort, irritation, maybe even *anger*.
4. It could express affection, anger, playfulness, control, status. . . . These are just a *few* functions of touch.
5. In **some** cultures, it is common to see same-sex friends holding hands and embracing in public. This behavior is not interpreted as sexual. However, think about this behavior in some **other** cultures. Is it appropriate?

Lecture Part 1 – Sarcasm and Proxemics

1 Guessing vocabulary from context Page 115

B

1. f	2. e	3. c	4. a
5. b	6. g	7. d	8. h

2 Summarizing what you have heard Page 116

C

Word choice will vary.

Strong emotions are usually conveyed nonverbally: by gestures, body posture, facial expressions, voice, eye contact, use of space, and touching. Sometimes we rely completely on nonverbal cues [body language] to communicate. At other times, nonverbal cues add to the meaning of the words that we use.

One good example of the second case is seen in our use of humor and sarcasm. Often, in making a joke, Americans will say the opposite of what they mean. The only way to know what they really mean is to understand [pay attention to, read] the nonverbal [subtle] cues that go along with their words. These could be their tone of voice or a facial expression.

An important area of communication is *proxemics*, the study of personal space. Each of us has a "body bubble" around us. Its size depends on several factors, such as our relationship with the people around us, the social context, and our gender. If someone enters our personal space [bubble], we will become aware of it [possibly feel uncomfortable]. Culture also plays an important role in proxemics; some cultures – for example, Latin American [Middle Eastern] have smaller bubbles than others.

Lecture Part 2 –Touch

1 Guessing vocabulary from context Pages 116–117

B

1. h	2. f	3. j	4. i	5. c
6. d	7. a	8. g	9. e	10. b

2 Summarizing what you have heard Page 117

C

Word choice will vary.

Another important form of <u>nonverbal communication</u> is <u>touch</u>. As with space, rules of <u>touch</u> are very subtle, and they are mostly determined by <u>gender</u> and <u>culture</u>. What is acceptable in one culture may be <u>taboo</u> [<u>unacceptable</u>, <u>wrong</u>] in another culture. For example, in China, <u>friends of the same sex hold hands in public</u>. But in the United States, <u>they do not</u> [<u>this is considered sexual</u>].

In conclusion, we should remember that nonverbal <u>misunderstandings</u> [<u>mistakes</u>] do not often result in cross-cultural <u>problems</u> [<u>alienation</u>, <u>misinterpretation</u>, <u>anger</u>]. In fact, these mistakes can be a source of <u>humor</u> [<u>laughter</u>] and <u>camaraderie</u> [<u>good feeling</u>] between people of different cultures.

Unit 3 Academic Vocabulary Review

1 Word forms Pages 120–121

A

1. communicate; communication
2. emphasize; emphasis
3. interpretation; misinterpreted; Misinterpretation
4. function; functional
5. dimensions; dimensional
6. intensify; intensity; intense
7. violate; violation
8. contextual; context
9. complex; complexities
10. norms; normal

Chapter 7
Friendship

1 Getting Started

3 Listening for specific information Page 128
A

Otis – Tom – 1956 – Yale University
David – Douglas – 1982 – college (music classes)
Pam – Jeanette – 1981 – grade school [elementary school]
Tony – Hubert – 27 years ago – college (same classes)
Catherine – Odette – 1999 – graduate school
Ruth – Esther – 1996 – her synagogue

2 Real-Life Voices

Interview Part 1 – Starting friendships

2 Retelling Page 130
C

Word choice will vary.

1. They met when the interviewer interviewed Catherine for a teaching job. They became friends after Catherine asked the interviewer to help her give her cat a flea bath. It was difficult to do, but they had fun.
2. She values her job and takes teaching seriously. She finds that most of her friends have a similar attitude toward work [a similar work ethic]. She thinks that a shared work ethic is a good basis on which to build a friendship.
3. Catherine met Odette when they were in the same linguistics class in graduate school. She thought Odette looked like a really "cool" person and she wanted to be friends with her, but she thought Odette probably wouldn't like her. She was intimidated by Odette. Then they were in the same study group and started talking. Odette told her that she had felt the same way about Catherine, so they became close friends.

Interview Part 2 – Maintaining friendships

2 Retelling Page 131
C

Word choice will vary.

1. They worked together in the same place but didn't know each other very well. Then Doug moved overseas and they started writing letters to each other, and that is how they became friends. They've been corresponding for over 20 years.
2. Catherine uses Skype to keep in touch with her friend Corey, who lives in Chicago. She likes Skype because they can see each other, and she can see the room where he is sitting and say hi to his wife Misayo if she comes into the room. Sometimes she and Misayo will show each other what they have been knitting. Catherine even gets to see their dog Peanut. She feels as if she has just dropped in for a visit.

Interview Part 3 – What friends do for each other

2 Summarizing what you have heard Pages 131–132
B

Word choices will vary. Some alternatives are given in brackets.

According to Catherine, one of the most important things that friends can do for each other is call each other on things [let each other know when they are upset about something]. She believes that fighting is a way to show that you care. Other important things that friends give one another are comfort, support, adventure, and jokes.

Catherine's more recent friendships revolve around her son Leo; she thinks that being a parent is such an all-consuming [a powerful] experience that it bonds a person [bonds you] to people who are going through the same thing. However, she still maintains her old friendships, thanks to e-mail, letters [snail mail], the phone, and Skype.

Finally, Catherine says that friends are "the family we get to choose."

3 Listening for verb tense and aspect Page 132

A

1. b   2. c   3. c   4. a   5. c

4 Academic Listening and Note Taking

Before the Lecture

4 Using morphology, context, and nonverbal cues to guess meaning Pages 137–138

A

Notes will vary.

1. subject – ive (adjective ending)
2. social (adjective) network (noun)
3. loners: noun with -er ending = person; –s = people
4. vulner – able adjective – able to??
5. overscheduled -d ending = verb or adjective; over- = too much

B

Wording will vary.

1. subjective: "means different things to different people"
2. social network: support systems, family and friends
3. loners: people who are content to be alone
4. vulnerable: able to be hurt by something, like pain or rejection
5. overscheduled: always busy with some organized activity, going to piano lessons, football practice, ballet class, etc.

Lecture Part 1 – The Role of Friendship in Good Mental Health

1 Guessing vocabulary from context Pages 138–139

B

1. c 2. f 3. m 4. d 5. h 6. g 7. i
8. k 9. b 10. a 11. l 12. j 13. e

2 Listening for specific information Pages 139–140

C

Wording will vary.

1. A song titled "People" caused the lecturer to think about friendship. The song says that people who need other people are lucky.
2. Social networks are an important sign of how a person is getting along. A person needs to feel supported by family and friends.
3. Clients who have support systems are much less likely to commit suicide, and if clients are feeling suicidal, it is important for their friends and family to know it.
4. Friends may reject us.
5. They are afraid of – or tired of – being rejected. It's less painful to simply be a loner.

Lecture Part 2 – New Challenges to Friendship

1 Guessing vocabulary from context Pages 140–141

B

1. b 2. k 3. f 4. j 5. e 6. l
7. g 8. c 9. h 10. d 11. i 12. a

2 Listening for specific information Page 141

C

Wording will vary.

1. Many children are 'overscheduled' with lessons and activities. The lecturer says that children need unstructured time to develop friendships with other kids.
2. Adults spend a lot more time at work than in the past. So they have less time for family and friends. They may also leave friends and family and move to a different city if their work requires it.
3. It is replacing face-to-face interaction.
4. Social connectivity is not true friendship. It can help you maintain friendships that you already have, but it is not an effective way to make new friendships.

Chapter 8
Love

1 Getting Started

3 Listening for details Page 145
A

Notes will vary.

1. Les: librarian, divorced, late 30s, likes jazz, movies, museums, wants a match
2. Michael: M.D., works hard, climbs mts., 35, wants attractive, younger wm.
3. Alicia: wants kind, depend. man, gd. father; has 2 chldrn. (4 & 6), comput. engin.
4. Frank: Jr. HS tchr., likes garden'g., baseball, 37
5. Sara: artist, early 40s, shy, likes to talk abt. art & books
6. Suzanne: into health, mid 20s, wants mature man, rich

2 Real-Life Voices

Interview Part 1 – Courtship

2 Listening for specific information Page 147
B

Wording will vary.

1. 33 years
2. Ann was a senior in high school (16) and Jim was a senior in college.
3. She thought he was the best person she had ever met.
4. She was afraid that Jim would marry her older sister.
5. 11 years
6. A friend warned him that Ann was thinking of marrying someone else, so he drove to her home and asked her mother for permission to marry Ann.
7. She feels fortunate that she didn't give up and marry someone else during the 11 years that it took Jim to propose.

Interview Part 2 – Making marriage work

2 Listening for specific information Pages 147–148
B

Wording will vary.

1. They have both done interesting things in their lives, and they are proud of one another's accomplishments.
2. classical music, living in other countries and learning about other cultures, gardening, walking, family, church
3. Ann is good at financial management and keeping records, and Jim is not.
4. They respect each other.
5. working overseas, living in a tent in the Somalian desert for three months, raising their two boys: These experiences have sometimes been difficult, but they have bonded Ann and Jim.

3 Listening for digressions Page 149
A

1. but at age 16
2. my greatest fear
3. Aunt Amy called up
4. and I asked her mother

4 Academic Listening and Note Taking

Before the Lecture

2 Taking advantage of rhetorical questions Page 156
A

1. asking for information
2. opinion
3. opinion
4. asking for information
5. asking for information
6. asking for information

Lecture Part 1 – The Matching Hypothesis

1 Guessing vocabulary from context   Page 157

B

1. d	2. l	3. g	4. h	5. i	6. k
7. e	8. c	9. f	10. j	11. b	12. a

2 Outlining practice   Page 158

D

Notes will vary.

I. the matching hypothesis = we tend to be attracted to people who are like us
  A. possible areas of similarity
    1. physical
      e.g., a "five" is probably going to marry a "five," not a "ten"
    2. personality
    3. job
    4. similar intelligence
    5. education
      e.g., college graduate who marries hs grad. – problems – too big a gap
    6. same interests
    7. same values
    8. religion
    9. race
    10. age: usually within 5–10 years
    11. socio-economic status

Lecture Part 2 – The Matching Hypothesis (cont.) and Other Theories

1 Guessing vocabulary from context   Page 159

B

1. b	2. d	3. h	4. g
5. c	6. a	7. f	8. e

2 Outlining practice   Pages 159–160

D

Notes will vary.

I. (cont.) The matching hypothesis, general rule: the ↑ similar you are, the ↑ likely to stay married.
  A. possible areas of similarity (cont.)
    politics – want pers. who validates our ideas
II. Complementarity = the idea that opposites attract – sometimes works in rel'ships e.g., submissive pers. is happier with a dominant pers. than w/ another sub. pers.
III. The Romeo and Juliet effect = more oppos. from parents, etc. → more attraction
IV. Conclusion: most import. idea = similarity – we are attracted to people like us

Unit 4 Academic Vocabulary Review

1 Word forms   Page 162

1. indicative; indicator; indicates
2. opposites; opposition
3. Maintaining; maintenance
4. assume; assumption
5. hypothesis; hypothesizes; hypothetically
6. validate; validity
7. complements; complementarity
8. dominant; dominate

Chapter 1 • Lecture Quiz

Answer the following questions on Parts 1 and 2 of the Chapter 1 lecture, "Stress and the Immune System." Use only the lecture notes that you took on your own paper to help you. Answer each question as fully as possible. You will receive 2 points for each complete and correct answer and 1 point for each partially correct answer.

1. Name two health problems referred to in the lecture that can be psychosomatic disorders, that is, that can be caused by psychological problems. (**2 points**)

2. What is psychoneuroimmunology? (**2 points**)

3. What did Ader discover by accident while experimenting on rats and why was his discovery important? (**2 points**)

4. Which group of elderly patients in nursing homes tends to be healthier and why? (**2 points**)

5. What are more and more doctors encouraging their patients to practice and why? (**2 points**)

Name: _____

Date: _____

Chapter 2 • Lecture Quiz

Answer the following questions on Parts 1 and 2 of the Chapter 2 lecture, "Risk Factors in Cardiovascular Disease." Use only the lecture notes that you took on your own paper to help you. Answer each question as fully as possible. You will receive 2 points for each complete and correct answer and 1 point for each partially correct answer.

1. What is happening when a person has a stroke? **(2 points)**

2. Who has more cardiovascular disease, men or women? Why? **(2 points)**

3. When a man in his thirties has a heart attack or stroke, what is the usual explanation? **(2 points)**

4. What is the connection between obesity and cardiovascular disease? **(2 points)**

5. Why is stress considered a risk factor for cardiovascular disease? **(2 points)**

Chapter 3 • Lecture Quiz

Answer the following questions on Parts 1 and 2 of the Chapter 3 lecture, "Erik Erikson's Fifth Stage of Psychosocial Development: Adolescence." Use only the lecture notes that you took on your own paper to help you. Answer each question as fully as possible. You will receive 2 points for each complete and correct answer and 1 point for each partially correct answer.

1. What does Erik Erikson mean by "identity versus role confusion?" **(2 points)**

2. What is physically challenging about adolescence? **(2 points)**

3. What is socially challenging about adolescence? **(2 points)**

4. According to the lecturer, what long-term effect does drug and alcohol use have on an adolescent? **(2 points)**

5. Why is the lecturer concerned about adolescent use of information technology? **(2 points)**

Chapter 4 • Lecture Quiz

Answer the following questions on Parts 1 and 2 of the Chapter 4 lecture, "Developmental Tasks of Early Adulthood." Use only the lecture notes that you took on your own paper to help you. Answer each question as fully as possible. You will receive 2 points for each complete and correct answer and 1 point for each partially correct answer.

1. What is considered to be the ideal relationship for parents and children in Western cultures once the children become young adults? (**2 points**)

2. Why are young people today living at home with their parents longer than young people did in the past? (**2 points**)

3. According to Erikson, what do partners need to be able to do in order for a marriage to succeed? (**2 points**)

4. According to the lecturer, why do some people choose isolation over intimacy? (**2 points**)

5. Why are young people waiting longer to get married than in the past? (**2 points**)

Chapter 5 • Lecture Quiz

Answer the following questions on Parts 1 and 2 of the Chapter 5 lecture, "Body Language Across Cultures." Use only the lecture notes that you took on your own paper to help you. Answer each question as fully as possible. You will receive 2 points for each complete and correct answer and 1 point for each partially correct answer.

1. Why is the lecturer surprised that experts say, "Somewhere between 60 and 90 percent of everything we communicate is nonverbal?" (**2 points**)

2. Name three things that people use to communicate nonverbally. (**2 points**)

3. Explain how eye contact in the United States and in Japan is different. (**2 points**)

4. Explain how the word *maybe* in Japanese, as an answer to a question asking for permission, can mean different things. (**2 points**)

5. At the end of the lecture, what does the lecturer say is important to do and interesting, too? (**2 points**)

Chapter 6 • Lecture Quiz

Answer the following questions on Parts 1 and 2 of the Chapter 6 lecture, "Nonverbal Communication – The Hidden Dimension of Communication." Use only the lecture notes that you took on your own paper to help you. Answer each question as fully as possible. You will receive 2 points for each complete and correct answer and 1 point for each partially correct answer.

1. What is sarcasm? How does it relate to the topic of the lecture? (**2 points**)

2. How do people react when someone violates their personal space? Name two specific possibilities. (**2 points**)

3. Name two factors that can influence the amount of space between two people who are communicating. (**2 points**)

4. Name three things that touch can express. (**2 points**)

5. Give an example from the lecture of touching behavior that is taboo in American culture. (**2 points**)

Chapter 7 • Lecture Quiz

Answer the following questions on Parts 1 and 2 of the Chapter 7 lecture, "Looking at Friendship." Use only the lecture notes that you took on your own paper to help you. Answer each question as fully as possible. You will receive 2 points for each complete and correct answer and 1 point for each partially correct answer.

1. Give two reasons why a therapist wants to know about the social networks of a person who is suicidal. **(2 points)**

2. What does the lecturer mean when he says that friendship can be a risky business? **(2 points)**

3. Why is it wrong to "overschedule" children, according to the lecturer? **(2 points)**

4. In what way is social networking good for friendship? **(2 points)**

5. Why is the lecturer concerned about Facebook? **(2 points)**

Name: _____

Date: _____

Chapter 8 • Lecture Quiz

Answer the following questions on Parts 1 and 2 of the Chapter 8 lecture, "Love – What's It All About?" Use only the lecture notes that you took on your own paper to help you. Answer each question as fully as possible. You will receive 2 points for each complete and correct answer and 1 point for each partially correct answer.

1. How would a sociobiologist explain the attraction that one individual might have for another? **(2 points)**

2. How does the matching hypothesis explain the fact that sometimes a beautiful woman loves an unattractive man, or a handsome man loves an unattractive woman? **(2 points)**

3. List five areas mentioned by the lecturer in which you might expect to find similarities between people who are attracted to each other. **(2 points)**

4. According to the lecturer, sometimes it is better for people in a relationship to have differences. Explain how the example that he gives illustrates this. **(2 points)**

5. Explain the Romeo and Juliet effect. **(2 points)**

Lecture Quiz Answer Keys

Chapter 1
1. Students should name two of the following: migraine headaches, high blood pressure, skin rashes, ulcers, heart disease.
2. It is the study of the connection between stress and illness or how the mind influences the functioning of the immune system.
3. He discovered that the immune system can be conditioned or taught to malfunction, which suggests that it can also be conditioned to get better.
4. Patients who choose to be in nursing homes tend to be healthier because they have some control over their lives; there appears to be a connection between health and feeling in control of one's situation.
5. They encourage them to practice relaxation techniques as a way to control certain medical conditions, such as headaches and sleeplessness.

Chapter 2
1. One or more arteries to the brain become blocked.
2. Men do. Women are protected by estrogen until menopause.
3. Family history, or heredity, is usually the explanation.
4. Obese people are more likely to develop diabetes and high blood pressure, which are both risk factors for cardiovascular disease.
5. Acute and chronic stress may lead to higher blood pressure and cholesterol, overeating, and smoking, all of which increase one's risk for cardiovascular disease.

Chapter 3
1. This is the psychosocial challenge that adolescents face; they need to establish their own identity, or sense of self, otherwise they will have problems making good choices as they get older.
2. Adolescents are growing very rapidly and their bodies are changing constantly. They are maturing sexually.
3. Adolescents are very self-conscious and very self-absorbed. They are very worried about being accepted by their peers.
4. Drug and alcohol use acts as a protective screen that prevents the teenager from facing reality, so if the adolescent uses drugs chronically, his or her social and emotional development is delayed.
5. We do not know what long-term effects information technology will have on children's psychological development; activities like computer games appear to have a hypnotizing effect.

Chapter 4
1. Children in their early twenties are expected to become independent from their parents in all ways: financially, emotionally, and socially.
2. It is more difficult today for young people to become financially independent because of greater job competition and the state of the economy.
3. They must be able to establish intimacy. This involves being willing and able to compromise, sacrifice, and negotiate.
4. They are afraid to open themselves up emotionally because they may be hurt. Often they have not established a strong identity in adolescence. Isolation is not a natural choice for humans.
5. Students should name two of the following reasons: less social pressure to marry young, greater desire to have the freedom to do other things, skepticism about marriage due to the high divorce rate.

Chapter 5

1. She is surprised because we usually focus so much attention on the words we choose when we express things. Most of us think that our use of words is very important in communication.
2. Students should name three of the following: body language, posture, gestures, facial expressions, eye contact, tone of voice, touch.
3. In the United States direct eye contact is normal and appropriate, but in Japan there is less direct eye contact. In the United States not looking someone directly in the eye is disrespectful, but in Japan this is not true.
4. Depending on the nonverbal cues, such as tone of voice and the gestures and posture that accompany the word *maybe*, it can mean either "maybe yes" or "definitely no."
5. She recommends that we study, observe, and pay close attention to our own patterns of body language and the body language of the people around us.

Chapter 6

1. Sarcasm is a form of humor in which nonverbal cues make it clear that the speaker really believes the opposite of what he or she is saying. Sarcasm relates to the topic of the lecture because it proves that nonverbal cues can carry the real meaning of a message.
2. They adapt their position in some way: turning, moving away, putting books in front of them, or closing their jackets.
3. Students should name two of the following: the degree of intimacy between them, the social context, their gender relationship, their culture.
4. Students should name three of the following: affection, anger, playfulness, control, status.
5. People of the same sex holding hands in public.

Chapter 7

1. (1) A person who has a strong network of friends has a lower risk of committing suicide. (2) A person's family and friends can help watch over that person and keep him or her safe.
2. When we make friends with someone, we risk being rejected by them, which can be very painful.
3. Children need free, unstructured time to develop friendships with other children. These friendships may last a lifetime.
4. Friends who are geographically separated can stay in touch using Skype, email, Twitter, or Facebook.
5. It is not the same kind of connection as face-to-face contact. It lacks intimacy.

Chapter 8

1. The sociobiologist would say that we are attracted to someone whom we unconsciously perceive as being a good genetic match in terms of his or her physical appearance and the kind of children he or she would produce.
2. The matching hypothesis states that we are attracted to people whom we see as being similar to us. Even though two people may not be equally attractive physically, they may have other similarities, such as common interests, level of education, etc.
3. Students should name five of the following: personality type, job, intelligence, level of education, interests, values, religion, race, age, socioeconomic status, political beliefs.
4. The lecturer says that a dominant person would probably get along better with a submissive person. If two submissive people lived together, they would have trouble deciding anything because they would each want the other person to decide everything.
5. As in the story of Romeo and Juliet, a couple will tend to feel more attracted to each other if there is opposition to their relationship from parents or friends.

Audio Script

Getting Started: Following directions, page 4

For this activity, first look at the graphic in your textbook. It shows a continuum from very relaxed at the far left to very stressed at the far right. Now stand up and move away from your desk. Find a big open space in the front or back of your classroom where you can imagine the same line going from left (very relaxed) to right (very stressed).

Or, if you prefer not to stand up, you can do the activity at your desk using the graphic in your book. You are going to hear a series of sounds, each preceded by a number. Listen carefully to each sound and pay attention to your body's reaction: Does it make you feel stressed? very stressed? relaxed? very relaxed? Or is it neutral for you, that is, neither stress-producing nor relaxing? As you listen, move to the space along the line that corresponds to your reaction. If you are sitting at your desk, write the number of the sound on the line in the place that corresponds to your reaction. Then wait for the next sound.

1. *(baby crying continuously)*
2. *(thunder and heavy rain)*
3. *(ocean waves breaking on the shore)*
4. *(loud laughter of children)*
5. *(a cat purring)*
6. *(a jet taking off)*
7. *(police sirens)*

Interview 1: The Stress of Teaching First-Graders
CD1 TR03 **Personalizing the topic, page 6**

Interviewer: Nancy, how long have you been teaching?

Nancy: Mmm, let's see, I've been teaching for 20 years now.

Interviewer: Twenty years!

Nancy: Yeah.

Interviewer: And have you always taught first grade?

Nancy: No, actually I've taught a variety of ages of children. Uh, I taught three-year-olds and preschool children for seven years, and then I taught fifth, fourth, and first grade at the elementary level.

Interviewer: So, always children.

Nancy: That's right.

Interviewer: Now, would you say that being an elementary school teacher was a stressful job?

Nancy: Yes, very much so.

Interviewer: And what is stressful about it?

Nancy: Well, the children bring a lot of problems into the classroom – problems from home, and then there are developmental things going on with each age, too – emotional and social, uh –

Interviewer: Could you think of, uh, an example of something stressful that happens at school? Y'know, something typical.

Nancy: Well, I guess when I'm trying to teach something new to a class of five- and six-year-olds, and that's about thirty-two students now, and you're trying to teach a new concept, and there's one disruptive child, and a lot of times lately there's been more than one disruptive child at a time who can't pay attention and is disturbing the children around him. So it pulls everyone off track.

Interviewer: So that you can't teach the lesson.

Nancy: Right. As a teacher, you feel it's your job to be teaching these things that are in the curriculum, and then you end up spending so much time trying to teach children how to get along in the classroom setting – and how to behave, and be polite to each other – and it seems like there gets to be less and less time to teach what we're supposed to be teaching.

Interviewer: OK, so there's less time for teaching and more time spent on –

Nancy: On helping children work out their personal problems.

Interviewer: Hmm. Now, Nancy, you say that teaching is very stressful. Do you think it's more stressful than other kinds of work? Have you had other jobs besides teaching that were –

Nancy: Yes, I've done office work and sales, and the big difference with teaching is that you're never really finished! I mean, when I did those other jobs, I could go home at five or whatever and forget about it till the next morning. But with teaching, it's never over until summer vacation.

Interviewer: Uh-huh.

Nancy: Y'know, I mean you carry around the responsibility of those children all the time.

Interviewer: So, evenings and weekends –

Nancy: Uh-huh, you are never really free of the stress of, of that responsibility.

Interviewer: Hmm. How does that stress manifest itself?

Nancy: Fatigue!

Interviewer: Fatigue? You feel tired a lot?

Nancy: Yeah. I think that comes with working with young children. And the younger the children you work with, the more energy they require. I think any mother of a young child will tell you that.

Interviewer: So you feel tired. Anything else? Do you ever lose your temper?

Nancy: Well, I have to keep my temper in the classroom. I mean, that's my job. But I do find that, um, now that I have a child of my own, I sometimes have less patience with him. And it's probably related to the fact that I've spent the whole day being very patient with 32 children! I mean, I have to admit that I'm a much better mother during the summer than I am during the school year.

Interviewer: Nancy, do you find that as a teacher you get sick more often than other people?

Nancy: Definitely! Especially when I was teaching preschool. Whatever cold or flu the children got, I would get, too.

Interviewer: Because of the stress of working with little kids? Or –

Nancy: Partly, yeah. I really believe that stress does make you more susceptible to illness, that it weakens your immune system. [*not completely certain of her facts*]

Interviewer: Mmm.

Nancy: Well, yeah! because . . . y'know, the younger the child, the closer you work with him, I mean, physically. I mean, y'know, the kids're in your lap, in your face, and they're coughing, sneezing, and touching you, and maybe your tolerance would be higher if you weren't under so much stress. I think it's related. [*said with confidence*]

Interviewer: Hmm. Nancy, what do you do to relieve stress?

Nancy: Well, I find it's very important to exercise. I, I go to an exercise class regularly.

Interviewer: Mmhm.

Nancy: Mmhm. And also it's been very important to me to have good friends that I can talk to when I need to.

CD1 TR04 ## Interview 1: The Stress of Teaching First-Graders
Listening for specific information, page 6

(Entire interview with Nancy is repeated.)

CD1 TR05 ## Interview 2: The Stress of Being a Police Officer
Listening for specific information, page 8

Interviewer: Sam, how long have you been a police officer?

Sam: I've been a police officer for 25 years.

Interviewer: Twenty-five years. And you've had different types of assignments on the police force?

Sam: Yeah, I've done everything – from patrol to undercover work to detective work, and now I'm supervising investigations.

Interviewer: Sam, I think most people would say that being a police officer is a very stressful job. Would you agree?

Sam: Yes, it's definitely a stressful job.

Interviewer: OK.

Sam: But of course it depends on your assignment.

Interviewer: So, what's probably the most stressful assignment you can have?

Sam: Uh, I'd say patrol is the most stressful assignment.

Interviewer: Interesting! In what way?

Sam: Well, I guess the biggest part of the stress is the fear factor – the fear of the unknown. In patrol work, you don't know from moment to moment who you are talking to or what their reaction is going to be to just your presence.

Interviewer: Hmm.

Sam: Let's say, for example, a patrol officer stops someone for a traffic violation. Now, it would seem as though that would be a very low-stress situation. But the truth is, there are more police officers stopped – pardon me – injured during a routine stop like that than in any other facet of police work.

Interviewer: Really?

Sam: Really! All police officers are taught from the very beginning that that is a time when they must be aware of their surroundings, of what the person in the car is doing, because they could be dead before they get back to their car. People back over policemen, people shoot policemen, people jump out at policemen – different things. So that's probably the most stressful time.

Interviewer: I see. Sam, how about the connection between stress and illness . . . do you think that there's a higher percentage of illness among police officers than in the general population? I mean, do they get more colds or anything? Is this really true?

Sam: Yes, definitely, and the stress level not only manifests itself, um, in daily health – whether or not you're feeling well on any given day. It also manifests itself in things like ulcers, heart disease – police officers tend to have a higher rate of heart disease and ulcers than people in other professions.

Interviewer: Really? That's documented?

Sam: Yes, it's documented. And also, the divorce rate among police officers is much higher.

Interviewer: Really? Is there something that the police department does to help you deal with this stress?

Sam: Yes, there are several programs that most police departments have in place. One is a physical training or exercise program – an established program where some part of your day is spent on some type of physical exercise. They've found that that's a great stress reducer. Um, there's also a psychological program with counseling for officers to help them reduce their stress. And there are several discussion groups. They've found that sometimes just sitting around and talking about the stress – with other officers – helps to reduce it. So, those things are available.

Interviewer: And what do you do, personally, to help you deal with the stress of your job?

Sam: Well, during the baseball season, I'm the biggest baseball fanatic, and I will either be reading about baseball, or listening to baseball, or watching baseball. Another thing I try to do is to get some sort of exercise every day. And then, I work hard at keeping my personal relationships, especially my relationship with my wife, at its peak. I'm very fortunate that I have a good relationship with my wife, and a good marriage. So when I come home, I can talk about my day with her, and then just forget about it.

CD1 TR06 ## Interview 2: The Stress of Being a Police Officer
Listening for tone of voice, page 8

1.

Nancy: I really believe that stress does make you more susceptible to illness, that it weakens your immune system. [*with slightly rising intonation, some doubt*]

Interviewer: Hmm.

2.

Interviewer: Mmm.

Nancy: Yeah, because . . . y'know the younger the child, the closer you work with him, I mean, physically. I mean, y'know, the kids're in your lap, in your face, and they're coughing, sneezing, and touching you, and maybe your tolerance would be higher if you weren't under so much stress. I think it's related. [*said with confidence*]

3.

Sam: All police officers are taught from the very beginning that that is a time when they must be aware of their surroundings, of what the person in the car is doing, because they could be dead before they get back to their car. People back over policemen, people shoot policemen, people jump out at policemen – different things.

4.

Sam: Police officers tend to have a higher rate of heart disease and ulcers than people in other professions.

Interviewer: Really? That's documented? [*surprised*]

CD1 TR07 ## In Your Own Voice: Asking for opinions, page 10
1.

Interviewer: Sam, I'd like your opinion. Which job would you consider more stressful, police officer or supervisor?

Sam: Oh, I'd have to say that, uh . . . [*fade out*]

2.

Interviewer: Nancy, I'm curious to know what you think. What do you think is the most stressful job anyone could have?

Nancy: Teaching! Well, I don't know if teaching is the MOST stressful job, but it's

3.

Interviewer: Sam, may I get your opinion? What kind of work do you think causes the most stress?

Sam: I think any job where you have to deal with the unexpected . . .

Lecture: Ellen Cash, "Stress and the Immune System"

CD1
TR08 **Before the Lecture: Using telegraphic language,** page 13

1. Think of people that you know with migraine headaches or high blood pressure, skin rashes, high cholesterol, heart disease. The list goes on and on. All of these symptoms may be related to psychosomatic disorders.
2. We have found through research that the efficiency of the immune system is compromised, d- damaged, by certain stressors, and we have support for this from two areas of research – both from humans and from animals.
3. We find that today it is widely accepted in the medical field . . . among health care professionals, that the mind has a powerful effect on the body, and that this effect is especially negative when a patient feels helpless, when he feels he has no control
4. . . . In the case of problems like headaches, uh, sleeplessness, um, even high blood pressure, more and more health care providers are teaching patients to control these by simple relaxation techniques, which can be very effective – more effective than medication.

Lecture Part 1: "Psychoneuroimmunology (PNI) and Animal Studies on Stress"

CD1
TR09 **Summarizing what you have heard,** page 15

It seems obvious that the mind will have an effect on the body, and in recent years, we've gathered some hard data that this is true, that the way that you think actually affects the way your body feels. Um, stress has real implications, in terms of what it can do to the body, and psychosomatic disorders, or disorders where there is a physical symptom caused by a psychological problem, is a real hot topic in psychology today, um, because it's the border between psychology and medicine and relevant to almost all areas of our lives. Think of people that you know with migraine headaches or high blood pressure, skin rashes, high cholesterol, heart disease. The list goes on and on. All of these symptoms may be related to psychosomatic disorders. What I want to focus on today is an area of research on stress and illness, and this field is called psychoneuroimmunology, or PNI for abbreviation. I suggest that you abbreviate it. The word psycho neuro immunology: psycho means the mind, the way that a person thinks; neuro is the nervous system; and immunology is the body's defenses against disease, the immune system. The immune system has two important tasks: basically to recognize foreign invaders, things that come into the body, and then to inactivate them and remove them from the body. We have found through research that the efficiency of the immune system is compromised, d- damaged, by certain stressors, and we have support for this from two areas of research – both from humans and from animals. And I'll start with some of the animal studies: So, we know that rats or mice that are placed in a situation where there was uncontrollable or unpredictable stress, uh – for example, shining bright lights on them or giving them electrical shocks to their feet or overcrowding them, which, you know, would be stressful – when these rats are infected with cancer cells and then placed in an environment

like that, they're much more likely to develop cancer under these stressful conditions than if they're in nonstressful conditions. Another really important study done with animals and immune functioning was done by a fellow named Robert Ader, and Ader was actually doing a study on taste aversion in rats when he discovered, quite by accident, that he was able to condition the rats' immune systems to malfunction. Now, this has very powerful implications because if we can teach the immune system, if, if we can condition it to malfunction, then it makes sense that we could also condition it to get better and to heal itself without medicine, and that's very exciting. And that's where we are now, in this research.

Lecture Part 2: "Human Research on PNI"

CD1
TR10 **Summarizing what you have heard,** page 18

And some of the studies on humans also support this idea that the mind can control the immune system. We know that people under great stress – when we analyze some of their immune functioning – we know that right before they experience a stressor, their immune systems become compromised – uh, for example, accountants before tax time or students before final exams. So if you think in terms of classical conditioning, y'know, like Pavlov and his experiments with dogs, in our case, the mental stress of just thinking about the exam or just thinking about being very busy at work is acting like, uh, like Pavlov's bell – acting as a conditioned stimulus to depress the immune system.

We find that today it is widely accepted in the medical field . . . among health care professionals, that the mind has a powerful effect on the body, and that this effect is especially negative when a patient feels helpless, when he feels he has no control. Um, elderly people in nursing homes. We know that, there was one study done on nursing home residents: one group of elderly people who felt that they were in control of their lives and they made the choice to be there; another group who felt that they were placed there by their family members, and who really didn't want to be there and they felt out of the control of the decision. Well, the ones who felt out of control were much more likely to get sick and to die, to lead unhealthy lives, while the ones who felt in control tended to be healthier.

And there's another way in which the mind can exert a positive influence on the body. . . . In the case of problems like headaches, uh, sleeplessness, um, even high blood pressure, more and more health care providers are teaching patients to control these by simple relaxation techniques, which can be very effective – more effective than medication. So, there's real exciting implications with this work and . . ., we're just beginning to understand how powerful the mind is in controlling the body.

Unit 1: Mind, Body, and Health
CD1
TR11 ## Chapter 2: Lifestyle and Health

Getting Started: Following directions, page 23

In this exercise, you are going to measure your heart rate, that is, how many times per minute your heart beats. It's very easy to measure your heart rate. You can feel it at several points on your body, for example, on your wrists or on either side of your neck. What you are feeling is called your pulse. What exactly is happening when we feel our pulse? When the heart beats, there is a short pause after each beat. During this pause, the blood is pushed through the arteries in our body. This movement of blood causes a kind of wave. And we can feel this wave at the points where arteries are close to the surface of the skin. We all know that our hearts beat faster when we are working hard physically. The reason for this is that our muscles need more oxygen in order to work, and oxygen is carried in the blood. Now let's see how our heart rates respond to the needs of our muscles. Sit quietly and relax. Just breathe normally, in and out. Take your right hand and, with the first two fingers, feel the side of your neck until you locate your pulse. Can you find it? Just keep your fingers resting lightly on your pulse. We're going to measure it for 15 seconds. When I say go, begin counting. Begin with zero, not one. Keep counting your pulse until I say stop. Are you ready? Go! [*long pause*] Stop. Now multiply the number of beats that you counted by four. That is your resting heart rate. Write it down in your book where it says first heart rate. Now we're going to see what effect a little exercise will have on your heart rate. I'm going to ask you to stand up and do some movements with your arms – first your right arm, then your left, then both – either up, forward (that is, in front of you), or to the side. After each movement, bring your arms back to your sides. Be sure that you have enough room to put your arms out to the side without hitting your classmates. Now I want you to use a lot of energy. Really move those arms. OK? Are you ready? Right arm first. Here we go. Right arm **up**, now left arm **up**, now both arms **up**. Remember to bring your arms back to your side each time. Again, right arm **up**, now left arm **up**, now both arms **up**. Now forward **right**, forward **left**, both forward. Again – forward **right**, forward **left**, **both** forward. Now to the side **right**, to the side **left**, to the side **both**. Again to the side **right**, to the side **left**, to the side **both**. Now both arms **up**, down, again **up**, down, again **up**. Again both arms **up**, down, again **up**, down, again **up**. Now both arms forward, again forward, again forward. Again both arms **forward**, again forward, again forward. Now to the **side**, again **side**, again **side**. Again to the **side**, **again** side, again side, and **stop**. Good work! Find your pulse on the side of your neck and let's get ready to count beginning with zero. Ready? Go! [*long pause*] Stop. Now multiply by four, and write down your second heart rate in your book. Subtract and find your increase.

Interview 1: Starting Smoking and Trying to Quit

CD1 TR12 **Anticipating answers,** page 25

Interviewer: Pat, I understand that you used to smoke. Is that correct?

Pat: Yes, that's right.

Interviewer: When did you start?

Pat: I started when I was probably, what, 13, 14.

Interviewer: Hmm! And how did you smoke?

Pat: I smoked heavily for about, uhh, 20 years on cigarettes, and then I switched to a pipe and smoked a pipe for about, uh, five years.

Interviewer: And, uh, why did you start smoking in the first place? That's kind of young.

Pat: It was cool.

Interviewer: Were your friends smoking?

Pat: Yeah, you know, peer pressure, that kind of –

Interviewer: What did your parents say about it?

Pat: Oh, they tried to make me quit from time to time, but it never did any good.

Interviewer: Uh-huh. Now how much, how much did you smoke? How many cigarettes a day?

Pat: Um, at the peak, 20 to 30 – a pack and a half.

Interviewer: So, now, you started when you were about 13, and you smoked for 25 years, did you say?

Pat: Right.

Interviewer: Twenty-five years! And, uh, did you ever try to quit?

Pat: Oh, yes. I tried several times.

Interviewer: What method did you use to try to quit?

Pat: Just willpower.

Interviewer: Did you ever succeed for a short time?

Pat: Oh, for days at a time.

Interviewer: Hmm.

Pat: Well, my senior year in high school, I played basketball, and my coach convinced me that I'd play better if I quit smoking, so I quit smoking for the season.

Interviewer: Hmm!

Pat: And the day after we lost our last game, I, uh, started up again [*laughs*].

Interviewer: [*laughs*] Back to the cigarettes, huh?

Pat: Yeah.

Interviewer: Well, uh, so how did you finally quit?

Pat: Uh, when was that? About, um, 1998 I think.

Interviewer: 1998.

Pat: Right. I had a heart attack, and they wouldn't let me smoke in the hospital.

Interviewer: [*gasps*] A heart attack!?

Pat: Yeah, and while I was in the hospital, my wife threw away all my tobacco and pipes and, by the time I got home, I wasn't hooked anymore.

Interviewer: So, do you mean you've never been tempted to start smoking again?

Pat: No! In fact, I dream about it every once in a while, and it's more like a nightmare.

Interviewer: Ahhh.

Pat: I wake up thinking, "Oh, no! I didn't start again, did I?"

Interviewer: I'm wondering how quitting affected your health . . . did you notice any big differences?

Pat: Oh, yeah! . . . I just had a lot more energy, my breathing got a lot easier . . .

Interviewer: Hmm.

Pat: . . . all kinds of things, uh, walking, biking, . . . singing, running. . . . My son and I were doing a lot of backpacking during that time, and that got a lot easier after I stopped smoking . . .

Interviewer: Hmm.

Pat: . . . food tastes a lot better.

Interviewer: Did you gain weight?

Pat: Um-hmm. About 30 pounds, I guess.

Interviewer: Uh, so, Pat, uh, what advice would you give to someone who's trying to quit?

Pat: [*laughs*] To have a heart attack? Hmm, uh, seriously, uh, I wouldn't. I really wouldn't.

Interviewer: You wouldn't give advice?

Pat: Nope. So many people gave me advice. I gave myself so much advice, and to me, it was meaningless. Uh, you have to decide for some reason or another that you really wanna quit, and then you will.

Interview 2 Part 1: Quitting Smoking

CD1 TR13 **Paraphrasing what you have heard,** page 27

Interviewer: I'm talking with Donna, a former smoker. When did you start smoking cigarettes, Donna?

Donna: I started when I was about 16 or 17 years old. It was kind of a cool thing to do. A lot of my friends would get together after school in a public park and sit around and talk and smoke and eat candy –

Interviewer: Did your parents know about it?

Donna: Oh, no! They would've been so mad if they'd known.

Interviewer: How much did you, uh, smoke? Uh, how many –

Donna: Umm, at first, just five or six cigarettes a day, but then soon after that I went up to about a pack a day.

Interviewer: Hmm.

Donna: And, umm, I continued to smoke for another, y'know, 13 years. In high school I, um, traveled. I lived in South America as an exchange student, and, uh, it was very common for people to smoke there.

Interviewer: Uh-huh. More so than in the United States?

Donna: Yeah. People would smoke inside movie theaters, at school. And, then later I was teaching in Mexico, and I would smoke while I was teaching.

Interviewer: Interesting.

Donna: Yeah, and students would smoke, y'know, we'd pass cigarettes around the classroom.

Interviewer: Huh.

Donna: And people smoked in supermarkets, in taxicabs, in public buses.

Interviewer: Hmm. So, at what point did you think about quitting?

Donna: I think I started considering it really quite soon . . . after I became . . . I probably became fully addicted a year or two after I started. Maybe a year or two after that I started having problems with coughing, and when I was in Mexico, I started getting bronchitis . . .

Interviewer: Umhmm.

Donna: . . . and right after I got over it, I'd get it again.

Interviewer: Uh-huh.

Donna: Like, uh, I had chronic bronchitis –

Interviewer: Uh-huh.

Donna: And, um, I, I started trying to quit then, but I just couldn't.

Interviewer: Now, when you tried to quit, did you try any particular method? Or –

Donna: Initially, I just, I just went cold turkey: I just decided not to buy any more. And that didn't work, so then I tried the candy method.

Interviewer: The candy method?

Donna: Oh, I ate candy every time I wanted a cigarette, and that didn't work.

Interviewer: Did you gain weight?

Donna: Uh, I never went long enough.

Interviewer: [*laughs*]

Donna: I always started smoking again within two days, maybe, and it was really painful when I stopped smoking. I wouldn't sleep at night.

Interviewer: You mean when you were trying to quit.

Donna: . . . I experienced withdrawal. . . . Later, when I was pregnant, I cut back so I was hardly smoking at all, but that was really, really painful. I remember the first thing I did in the hospital after my son was born [*chuckles*] was go out in the hall and have a cigarette.

Paraphrasing what you have heard, page 29

Interviewer: I wanted to ask you, Donna: Were you experiencing social pressure to quit?

Donna: Yeah, when I came back to the States, there was pressure to quit. People would really, y'know, react negatively, especially if I was around their kids.

Interviewer: Uh-huh.

Donna: I remember one occasion going to the zoo with other parents – friends of mine, and their kids, and lighting up a cigarette at the zoo – outside, and everyone disappeared, including my friends and my sister, and they were looking at me really negatively – my own friends and sister. They didn't want their kids around it even outside.

Interviewer: Hmm . . . so how did you finally quit?

Donna: Well, I had a friend who had had a three-pack-a-day habit. And he told me about this woman who, um, hypnotized him, and he quit, and there was no pain at all! And so I just decided to give it a try.

Interviewer: And it worked?

Donna: Yeah, it worked for me – by the end of the fourth treatment, I had completely lost the urge to smoke, and it's never come back – this was like five years ago.

Interviewer: Hmm.

Donna: I had never been hypnotized before, but it was very effective. I was really impressed.

Interviewer: Why do you think this method finally worked for you after you'd tried so many times to quit?

Donna: I think, y'know, it was a combination of the method, and y'know, just being completely fed up with it. I just had to reach the point where I was just . . . ready to give up cigarettes.

Interviewer: Uh-huh. Now, your son. How old is he now?

Donna: He's 12.

Interviewer: Now, what are you gonna do if he starts smoking?

Donna: Y'know, he hated it when I smoked – he hated the smell, he was afraid for my health. He used to put messages in my cigarette pack in my pocket saying, "Quit smoking, Mom," so that when I'd smoke I'd find them.

Interviewer: Yeah?

Donna: And so I find it really hard to imagine that he would smoke. . . . But . . . yeah, what would I do . . . Well, . . . I would do everything in my power to educate him on the health hazards of smoking. I think any intelligent person who understands the health consequences of smoking will want to quit.

Interviewer: Uh-huh.

Donna: And I would like him to know that before he gets addicted.

Interviewer: Yeah. Now, can I ask . . . how do you feel physically? How did you feel after you quit?

Donna: I felt an immediate, immediate improvement in my energy level and health, and my general functioning, y'know . . .

Interiewer: No more bronchitis?

Donna: The bronchitis disappeared almost immediately, and my lung function improved dramatically. But the big thing I noticed is I just had so much more energy.

Interviewer: Huh.

Donna: And the second thing I noticed was smells. My sense of smell came back, and I really liked being able to smell things again.

Interviewer: Did food taste better?

Donna: Food tasted much better! Yeah, and I didn't gain much weight – I know some people do, but I just gained about five pounds, and then I started exercising, so that kept my weight in control and improved my metabolism. And I've just kept exercising, so I feel so much healthier.

Interviewer: Anything else you wanna add?

Donna: The money!

Interviewer: Ah!

Donna: Uh, cigarettes are really expensive. When I quit, I calculated exactly how much it would cost to smoke for a year – and when I quit, I put the money in a savings account. And at the end of one year, I went out and bought myself and my son mountain bikes to celebrate our anniversary.

Interviewer: That's great.

Donna: And I've just kept doing that, and every year, I use the money for something active and healthy to make our lives more fun.

Interview 2 Part 2: How Quitting Smoking Changes Your Life

CD1 TR15

Drawing inferences, page 30

1.

Pat: Well, my senior year in high school, I played basketball, and my coach convinced me that I'd play better if I quit smoking, so I quit smoking for the season.

2.

Pat: . . . food tastes a lot better.

Interviewer: Did you gain weight?

Pat: Mmhm. About 30 pounds, I guess.

3.

Interviewer: Now, your son . . . what are you gonna do if he starts smoking?

Donna: Y'know, he hated it when I smoked – he hated the smell, he was afraid for my health. He used to put messages in my cigarette pack in my pocket saying, "Quit smoking, Mom," so that when I'd smoke I'd find them.

4.

Donna: Later, when I was pregnant, I cut back so I was hardly smoking at all . . .

In Your Own Voice: Asking for confirmation, page 32

CD1 TR16

Interviewer: Pat, I understand that you used to smoke. Is that correct?

Pat: Yes, that's right.

Interviewer: So, now, you started when you were about 13, and you smoked for 25 years, did you say?

Pat: Right.

Pat: And the day after we lost our last game, I, uh, started up again. [*laughs*]

Interviewer: [*laughs*] Back to the cigarettes, huh?

Pat: Yeah.

Pat: Right. I had a heart attack, and they wouldn't let me smoke in the hospital.

Interviewer: [*gasps*] A heart attack!?

Pat: Yeah, and while I was in the hospital . . .

Pat: . . . by the time I got home, I wasn't hooked anymore.

Interviewer: So, do you mean you've never been tempted to start smoking again?

Pat: No! In fact, I dream about it . . .

Lecture: Kristine Moore, "Risk Factors in Cardiovascular Disease"

CD1 TR17

Before the Lecture: Using symbols and abbreviations, page 35

1. By cardiovascular disease, I mean heart attacks, strokes, and peripheral vascular disease.

2. Males appear to be at a higher risk for cardiovascular disease than females.

3. Obesity technically means at least 20 percent above ideal weight. Clearly, this puts a person at increased risk for diabetes and high blood pressure.

4. What may be happening is that acute and chronic stress results in higher blood pressure and cholesterol levels, more smoking, overeating, etc. – all of which are direct risk factors for cardiovascular disease.

Lecture Part 1: "Unalterable Risk Factors in CVD"

CD1 TR18

Outlining practice, page 38

Today I'm going to be speaking on risk factors for cardiovascular disease. By cardiovascular disease, I mean heart attacks, strokes, and peripheral vascular disease, which is also known as clots to the legs. When the arteries become diseased, there's a loss of elasticity so that the arteries are not as flexible as they used to be. There can also be partial or complete blocking of the arteries. When a person has a heart attack, what happens is there's a partial or complete blocking of one or more of the arteries which feed the heart muscle. In a stroke, we're talking about the blocking of one or more of the arteries which feed the brain. In peripheral vascular disease, again, also known as clots to the legs, there's a partial blockage of one or more of the arteries to usually one of the legs. Now, there are risk factors which do give us an idea of who might develop one of these problems or these diseases. Some of the risk factors are alterable. That is, that the person at risk can actually do something about them. And then there are some risk factors which are unalterable. I'm going to run through the unalterable ones first and then the alterable ones second. OK, the unalterable risk factors are number one: gender. Males appear to be at a higher risk for cardiovascular disease than females, at least up until 50 years of age. The simplest explanation is that estrogen, a hormone which is made in women's bodies up until menopause, appears to protect women from cardiovascular disease. Second, age. As a person ages, their risk of getting cardiovascular disease increases. There's not much we can do about aging, but that is a factor – that the older a person is, the higher their risk for cardiovascular disease. Third, diabetes. People with diabetes have a higher rate of cardiovascular disease. It's not known why, but unfortunately the statistics support this. And then, family history. We all have, and need to have certain amounts of fats and fatty acids that our bodies use metabolically, and as long as our cholesterol and some of these other fat-containing chemicals in the blood are kept in good, low, balanced way, they create no increased risk to a person. However, if they get to be in higher levels than is healthy, they can create a higher risk for cardiovascular disease. And this is to some extent hereditary. In fact, when you hear about youngish men, let's say men in their thirties who have heart attacks or strokes, usually it's because of family history. I mean, even if they have other risk factors, having a heart attack in one's thirties is very rare, and the cause is usually hereditary. So, those are the unalterable risk factors for cardiovascular disease.

Lecture Part 2: "Alterable Risk Factors in CVD"

** Outlining practice,** page 39

CD1
TR19
The alterable risk factors for cardiovascular disease include, first of all, high blood pressure. High blood pressure, again, does tend to run in families, but there are some very, very good medications that people can take that have very few side effects in order to control high blood pressure. High blood pressure often occurs in people who are obese, um, very overweight. But then there are many otherwise healthy people who simply have high blood pressure. And the important thing is to get these people on an appropriate medication, usually a combination of medications, and keep their blood pressure within a healthy range, and that will decrease their risk of cardiovascular disease. Next, obesity. A very high percentage of Americans are considered obese. Obesity technically means at least 20 percent above ideal weight. Clearly, this puts a person at increased risk for diabetes and high blood pressure, and so it's very important to get rid of that excess weight. However, if I knew how to cure obesity, I would be an extremely wealthy woman. It's a very, very complex disease process. Generally, a low-fat diet is recommended for people who are obese. Next, cigarette smoking is clearly a risk factor for cardiovascular disease. People who smoke cigarettes have more heart attacks and strokes and peripheral vascular disease, you know, blood clots in the legs. Clearly, they have a higher incidence of these diseases earlier in life, than nonsmokers. Tobacco use not only raises blood pressure, but it probably affects the way fats are metabolized as well. And then, psychosocial factors, and this would include social isolation, certain personality traits, and of course daily stress, like a high-pressure work situation; the evidence suggests that these factors put a person at increased risk for cardiovascular disease. However, more research is needed to understand how stress contributes to risk for heart disease. We're not sure whether stress directly contributes to increased risk for cardiovascular disease. What may be happening is that acute and chronic stress results in higher blood pressure and cholesterol levels, more smoking, overeating, etc., all of which are direct risk factors for cardiovascular disease. And then finally, sedentary lifestyle is the last factor to be added to the list of alterable risk factors for cardiovascular disease. People who do not exercise, even if they have low blood pressure, are not obese, do not have diabetes, are female, don't smoke cigarettes, are young, control their stress, and eat a low-fat diet, people who, even if all those factors are in their favor, if a person does not exercise, they increase their chances of cardiovascular disease. So, there we go – another good reason to exercise.

Unit 2: Development Through Life

CD2
TR01
Chapter 3: The Teen Years

Getting Started: Recording numbers, page 49

We all know from experience that children grow up at different rates, both physically and emotionally. Physically, gender accounts for the most significant difference in growth rates. In general, men end up taller than women, but that's not how it begins. Girls usually enter adolescence earlier. They start to get taller, and their bodies begin to mature sexually before boys' do. We're going to make a graph showing typical growth patterns for adolescent boys and girls. You'll draw one line for James, a boy, and a second for Sarah, a girl. Now, to make this graph, you'll need two different colored pens or pencils, or one pen and one pencil. Before we begin, complete the key next to the graph to show which pen or pencil will be for James's growth and which

for Sarah's growth. Are you ready? Look at the graph. As you listen, make points on your graph. Later, after you finish, you can connect the points with a line. We'll begin with James. When James was 10 years old, he was 4 feet, 10 inches. He grew slowly until the age of 14, when he reached 5 feet, 1 inch. Then he began to grow taller very quickly. By age 16, he was 5 feet, 8 inches tall. By 18, he was 5 feet 11. He continued to grow taller, and by age 21, James was 6 feet tall. He reached his full adult height, 6 feet, 1 inch, at the age of 22. Now take a moment to connect the points on your graph. Now you have a record of James's adolescent growth.

OK, now let's record Sarah's growth. Sarah was 4 feet, 9 inches at age 10. Then she began to grow taller at a rapid rate. By age 12, she was 5 feet, 4 inches. Her growth continued, and she reached 5 feet, 8 inches by the age of 15. She continued to grow, but more slowly. By age 18, she had reached her adult height of 5 feet, 9 inches. Now connect the points which represent Sarah's height at different ages.

Interview 1: Being a Teenager in a Different Culture

CD2
TR02
Listening for specific information, page 52

Interviewer: Pegah, how long have you been in the U.S.?
Pegah: A year and a half.
Interviewer: And your family is here?
Pegah: Yes, I'm here with my mother and my brother; my father's job is in Iran – but he comes here for vacation.
Interviewer: And you came here to study English after you graduated from high school?
Pegah: Yes.
Interviewer: OK. So you are 19. Would you say that your parents give you . . . enough freedom to do what you want?
Pegah: That is a good question. You know in Iran, emm, young people, at least girls, usually don't go out alone . . .
Interviewer: Uh-huh.
Pegah: . . . so if I wanted to go anywhere, usually I had to go with my parents. . . .[*laugh*] It's ok . . . it's good! [*laugh*] You know, if you grow up with this religion, you're comfortable with that.
Interviewer: Yes!
Pegah: Yeah. But . . . when I came here, I saw that this was a different culture. And when I told my father that, he understood. So now sometimes he says it's ok for me go out alone, but only if I am careful – for example, don't talk to people I don't know, don't go somewhere that could be dangerous.
Interviewer: Uh-huh.
Pegah: I'm 19, and I know what behavior my father expects, so if I want to go to a casino, I know what my father will say, so I don't even ask.
Interviewer: And he trusts you to follow his rules when you go out.
Pegah: Yeah. He'll say, "Yes, you can go, but leave your cell phone on, and if it rings, you have to pick up," so this is a good system.
Interviewer: Mmhm.
Pegah: But my father still worries about me being alone. That is the one reason my mother is still here with me; my father says to her, "Pegah will be lost without you! She needs you." He's always saying that!!! . . . [*conspiratorial*] But yesterday, I talked with my father, and he said, "If you get your driver's license, I'm going to take your mom back to Iran with me next time I visit." So . . . that's great! I'm gonna start studying to get my driver's license.

Interviewer: Well, your dad probably misses your mom!

Pegah: [*both laugh*] Yeah, exactly!

Interviewer: . . . You must miss your friends in Iran.

Pegah: Yeah, it's very hard when you come here, especially at my age. Before I came here, I thought, "Oh I'm sure I will meet some Iranian girls" . . . but, there aren't any, . . . and . . . it's really hard.

Interviewer: Do you think that because you do not have Iranian friends here, that makes your relationship with your mother stronger?

Pegah: Mmm, not really, because our relationship was always very close. Sometimes if I am very sad, I tell my mom . . . because if I don't tell her, I'll feel worse. If you talk with someone, it really helps.

Interviewer: So, Pegah, how are American teenagers different from teenagers in Iran?

Pegah: Well, one thing, you know, in my country, children stay with their parents until they are married.

Interviewer: And in the U.S., they usually can't wait to move out and be on their own . . . what do you think about that?

Pegah: Mmm . . . you know, sometimes I'd like to be more independent. I mean, of course I need my family to support me, but sometimes . . . well, I think about my father's experience . . . when he was 19, he came here by himself to go to school, and he didn't have any money.

Interviewer: Wow!

Pegah: Yeah. When he described this experience to us, it sounded really bad. And two years later, his younger brother came to the U.S., too, and he had to protect him.

Interviewer: Hmm.

Pegah: But he survived, and it gave him the self-confidence to be successful. And now, he always tells my brother and me, "You have to learn to depend on yourself." He's right, I think.

Interviewer: Hmm! So how is your relationship with your brother?

Pegah: Sometimes . . . he and I have some disagreements.

Interviewer: Yeah?

Pegah: Yeah, a little bit. You know, [*laugh*] he's three years older than me . . .

Interviewer: Is he overprotective?

Pegah: Yeah, sometimes [*laughing*] If I want to go out, he asks me, "Where are you going? Who are you going with?" You know, just like he's my dad . . .

Interviewer: So what do you say?

Pegah: [*laughing*] I say, "Dad already gave me permission, so why are you asking me?" . . . Sometimes I think to myself, it would be so nice to have a sister!

Interviewer: [*laughing*] . . . So when your mother goes back to Iran, what will it be like to live with your brother?

Pegah: Well, actually, we already have lived alone together. . . . My mother was back in Iran for a vacation last year. So we were alone for two months. You know, he's a very serious boy, so before my mom went, I was afraid it would be terrible to be alone with him, but after she left, he was very nice.

Interviewer: Oh!

Pegah: I didn't know how to cook, and we had to eat, so my mom would call and try to tell me how to cook things, but I wasn't very good, and the food was terrible! [*laughing*]

Interviewer: But your brother ate it anyway?

Pegah: Yeah! He didn't complain. . . . And there was another thing. I cannot stay at home all the time. I need to go out every day – maybe shopping or for a walk. But my brother's very different – he would be happy to stay home all the time. But when my mother was gone, he went out with me every day.

Interviewer: Because he knew you wanted to go out?

Pegah: Yeah!

Interviewer: One last question, Pegah, what are your future plans?

Pegah: Well, first I want to learn English, then I want to study to be a dentist . . .

Interviewer: Ahh!

Pegah: . . . because we really need good dentists in Iran.

Interview 2: Starting a New Life in One's Teens

CD2 TR03

Completing multiple-choice items, page 53

Interviewer: So, Anastassíya, you came to the U.S. when you were . . . 16, with your mother and . . .

Anastassiya: And my younger sister.

Interviewer: And how old is she?

Anastassiya: She's 13 now.

Interviewer: Thirteen. So . . . when you came here, you started high school?

Anastassiya: Yeah, I went to high school for one year, but then they canceled the ESL program and . . . I couldn't pass my classes, like history and biology, . . . it was really hard for me because I didn't speak English very well . . . so I decided to go to college – to take an ESL program to learn English.

Interviewer: Really?

Anastassiya: Yeah, I dropped out of high school . . . and took an English placement test for college.

Interviewer: . . . So . . . how was high school?

Anastassiya: Umm high school . . . it's . . . kind of a . . . terrible place because . . . I think it's the same in every country because students are . . . kind of trying to be grown up, and they're still teenagers, and everyone wants to look better than you and be better than you and . . .

Interviewer: Ah.

Anastassiya: And also, if you don't speak English, . . . it's kind of hard because the other students . . .

Interviewer: So the American students were . . .

Anastassiya: Not the American students – the American students were very kind and patient . . . but students from other countries who came here, maybe five years ago or seven years ago . . .

Interviewer: Yeah.

Anastassiya: And they can speak English very well so they . . . well, you can experience discrimination . . .

Interviewer: Hmm.

Anastassiya: Yeah. And also, . . . in high school, a lot of students don't care about getting an education, it's like their parents said "you have to go to school" so they go to school, but they don't really want to learn, they don't concentrate, and they can sometimes distract you from learning, too.

Interviewer: But now in college, it's different?

Anastassiya: Yeah, the students are more serious, they want to learn. My friends and I . . . when we have free time, we like to sit in the library. . . . It sounds strange [*laughs*], but we just sit and talk and help each other with English and math. I really like it.

Interviewer: So . . . who do you hang out with here – who are your friends?

Anastassiya: At first, in high school, I didn't have friends, . . . but after a while, I started to hang out with Turkish people.

Interviewer: Yeah?

Anastassiya: 'Cuz they're . . . I feel like there's something similar in our . . . like . . . vision of the world, or something like that.

Interviewer: Hmm!

Anastassiya: So I always hung out with them, and they helped me with my homework and my English. And now I have new friends at college . . .

Interviewer: So are your friends of different nationalities?

Anastassiya: Yeah, several different . . . uh, like Vietnamese, Mexican, Filipino, Iranian . . .

Interviewer: Any Americans?

Anastassiya: Not yet, but I'm taking a regular math class now, and there're a lot of American people, so I think we're gonna be friends . . .

Interviewer: Anastassiya, when you first came here, what was it like . . . um . . . for you in your family? I mean . . . does your mother speak English?

Anastassiya: A little bit . . .

Interviewer: Yeah? So . . . less than you.

Anastassiya: Yes.

Interviewer: So . . . did you find yourself responsible for –

Anastassiya: Yes, kind of, for example, when we need to go to the bank or some place like that. Because . . . usually when you go to the clinic, for example, you have an interpreter. But the store or the bank – you have nobody to translate for you, and these are kind of important situations.

Interviewer: Yeah!

Anastassiya: And I know that I have to, like . . . I really have to concentrate and get everything right and not make any mistakes.

Interviewer: Yeah!

Anastassiya: And that's a lot of responsibility.

Interviewer: Yeah! And did that start right away when you first came here?

Anastassiya: Yeah, just after we came here.

Interviewer: So how did that feel to be . . . responsible, in a way, for your mother and sister, at that age?

Anastassiya: I didn't feel any pressure from my mom, but it felt like . . . I'm not a teenager anymore! . . . When I was living in Kazakhstan, I was like . . . carefree! I had no responsibilities . . . but now I have to help my mom, and it's like . . . Suddenly, I'm an adult.

Interviewer: Yeah! You arrived here and suddenly you had to be in charge

Anastassiya: . . . Yeah, I just have to do it.

Interviewer: Yeah.

Anastassiya: I have to help my family.

Interviewer: Does that feel good, to be able to do that?

Anastassiya: Yes. Sometimes I'm tired, and I think, "Oh my god, I have a headache," but . . . I feel like I'm really part of the family . . .

Interviewer: Yeah.

Anastassiya: . . . like I'm kind of equal with my mom, like we're friends.

Interviewer: She probably really appreciates your being . . . so responsible.

Anastassiya: Yes. She says, like, "I'm proud of you." [laughs]

Interviewer: Does your mother ever worry about you, for example, if you are with your friends?

Anastassiya: It depends on which friends.

Interviewer: Ah.

Anastassiya: Like, when I had friends in high school, she was always worried about me – she called me like ten times an hour. And I said, "Mom, I'm ok, don't worry." But now she says, "You know, I can trust your friends. I can see that they are good people."

Interviewer: That's great.

Anastassiya: I think moms know . . .

Interviewer: Yeah. . . . One final question: What are your future plans?

Anastassiya: I wanna be a music producer – at first, I wanted to be an artist, but everyone said you can't make a good living as an artist in America, so I decided ok, I'll do art as my hobby, and I'll be a music producer.

Interview 2: Starting a New Life in One's Teens

CD2
TR04
Uses of *like* in casual speech, page 54

1.
Anastassiya: . . . I couldn't pass my classes, like history and biology, . . . [*pause 5 seconds*]

2.
Anastassiya: . . . it's like their parents said, "You have to go to school," . . .

3.
Anastassiya: . . . when we have free time, we like to sit in the library . . .

4.
Anastassiya: I really like it.

5.
Anastassiya: I have to, like . . . I really have to concentrate.

6.
Anastassiya: . . . I feel like there's something similar . . .

7.
Anastassiya: . . . there's something similar in our . . . like . . . vision of the world . . .

8.
Anastassiya: . . . or something like that.

9.
Anastassiya: . . . in Kazakhstan I was like . . . carefree!

10.
Anastassiya: My mom called me like ten times an hour.

In Your Own Voice: Correcting or expressing a negative politely, page 56

CD2
TR05

Interviewer: Do you think that because you do not have Iranian friends here, that makes your relationship with your mother stronger?

Pegah: Mmm, not really, because our relationship was always very close.

Interviewer: So when your mother goes back to Iran, what will it be like to live with your brother?

Pegah: Well, actually, we already have lived alone together.

Interviewer: Anastassiya . . . does your mother speak English?

Anastassiya: A little bit . . .

Lecture: Susan Jenkins, PhD, "Erik Erikson's Fifth Stage of Psychosocial Development: Adolescence"

CD2
TR06

Before the Lecture: Using space to show organizational structure, page 58

I wanna mention some of the specific, more recent . . . challenges that adolescents face in Western culture – drugs and alcohol. There's tremendous pressure in this age group to make decisions about use of drugs and alcohol and other mind-altering substances – smoking cigarettes, and so forth. And what we know now – there's been a lot of study on this in the last several decades – is that people who start using substances that have brain effects are really at a disadvantage of . . . just for example, if a kid starts smoking marijuana at age 12, it stops the emotional growth . . . that comes from having to deal with experience . . . "naked" [*little laugh*] – the drug acts as a protective screen between you and the reality that you're trying to learn about and come to terms with, and so for kids who use it chronically, that aspect, that line of development . . . just stops, so when young people who, for example, use alcohol in their teens and then some time in their twenties are able to stop using alcohol, they discover – to their shock – that they still feel like they're 15, when they started using. This effect – this limitation of brain development – is now documented, and it makes life very difficult for these kids.

Another thing that's happening now in the last few years has to do with the amount of information that is instantly available because of the Internet and iPods and iPhones, and being able to have all kinds of distractions and instant conversations and information, and there are wonderful things about it, but also, we have no idea what the impact of that is on developing brains . . . we have no idea. Ever since the advent of television, this has been a point of discussion, and there has been lots of research on the impact of television on the development of child and adolescent brains – and when computer games – video games – came along, – it was even more of an issue because they are hypnotizing in a way that TV is not. . . . They involve the brain in such a way that kids are really hypnotized by the experience. On its face, it's not a problem, but these are environmental stimuli that in the past were not available to kids in the way that they are today, so we don't know about the impact on developing brains, and on psychological development. And again, I am not saying that they're bad, simply that we don't know about their long-term effects.

Lecture Part 1: "Adolescence: Identity versus Role Confusion"

CD2
TR07

Organizational structure, page 61

Ok, to review: we've been talking about psychologist Erik Erikson and his eight stages of psychosocial development, and you'll recall that each stage is expressed in terms of a conflict that ideally, the developing person resolves in order to move on to the next stage, so for example, the first stage, basic trust versus mistrust . . . this is a process that goes on for many years, but the establishment of basic trust happens from birth to about age two. So moving ahead, today we're looking at stage five, roughly the adolescent period, which covers about ages 12 to 16. Erikson's terms for this stage are identity versus role confusion, and the primary work of an adolescent in the psychosocial realm is to firmly establish their individual identity. If they are unable to do this, there's a danger of what Erikson called role confusion, or not being able to make good choices or even know what your choices are when it's very important to do so. There are a

few components to this work. One of the really big challenges of this period is that this is also the time of physical and genital maturation, which is terribly confusing for kids – it hardly matters what you tell them about what's gonna happen to their bodies, the experience of it and the rapidity of the physical growth is just really shocking. . . . You may have had the experience of not seeing someone who is 14 years old for a couple of months and when you see them again, they've grown six inches. And kids who are going through this are very, very self-absorbed . . . and worried about being socially accepted, so that in the midst of this physical change there is a demand socially and psychologically – by the individual and by the people around him or her – to grow up, to establish a psychological identity, ego identity, to be able to think beyond their own physical feelings and to keep hold of that basic trust that they're gonna make it through this period . . . and it is a really major challenge. And lots of kids hit the wall a few times before they actually feel confident and in control of their own direction, although most kids do make it through ok.

There's another, material challenge that arises in this work of establishing identity. And that . . . is making a choice about one's career, one's work. More and more kids successfully postpone this choice for a few years without too much worry by continuing their education. But even so, there's a surprising amount of anxiety that people have researched over the years in the area of career choice for adolescents.

And then, another big part of this work involves the whole question of falling in love . . . and gender identity. All of that comes way to the fore during this period, and it's important in terms of ego identity because finding someone who you can fall in love with brings up new aspects of yourself that didn't need to be touched before, and it's quite a dramatic change, and – one hopes that it's a wonderful change, but sometimes not – and in any case, very challenging.

Lecture Part 2: "Identity versus Role Confusion: New Challenges"

CD2
TR08

Organizational structure, page 63

I wanna mention some of the specific, more recent . . . challenges that adolescents face in Western culture – drugs and alcohol. There's tremendous pressure in this age group to make decisions about use of drugs and alcohol and other mind-altering substances – smoking cigarettes, and so forth. And what we know now – there's been a lot of study on this in the last several decades – is that people who start using substances that have brain effects are really at a disadvantage of . . . just for example, if a kid starts smoking marijuana at age 12, it stops . . . the emotional growth . . . that comes from having to deal with experience . . . "naked" [*little laugh*] – the drug acts as a protective screen between you and the reality that you're trying to learn about and come to terms with, and so for kids who use it chronically, that aspect, that line of development . . . just stops, so when young people who, for example, use alcohol in their teens and then some time in their twenties are able to stop using alcohol, they discover – to their shock – that they still feel like they're 15, when they started using. This effect – this limitation of brain development – is now documented, and it makes life very difficult for these kids.

Another thing that's happening now, in the last few years, has to do with the amount of information that is instantly available because of the Internet and iPods and iPhones, and being able to have all kinds of distractions and instant conversations and information, and there are wonderful things about it, but also, we have no idea what the impact of that is on developing brains . . . we have no idea. Ever since the advent of television, this has been a point of discussion, and there has been lots of research on the impact of television on the development of child and adolescent brains – and when computer games – video games – came along, – it was even more of an issue because they are hypnotizing in a way that TV is not. . . . They involve the brain in such a way that kids are really hypnotized by the experience. On its face, it's not a problem, but these are environmental stimuli that in the past were not available to kids in the way that they are today, so we don't know about the impact on developing brains, and on psychological development. And again, I am not saying that they're bad, simply that we don't know about their long-term effects.

Another thing to realize about adolescents is that they are experiencing their first true autonomy, being able to go out on their own without adult protection all the time, and they're seeking stimulation. . . . It's not as if they're trying to be careful; they are trying to be stimulated. They will take risks, and they will seek stimulation until they either have a problem, or a car wreck, or come to their own realization as to what they need to focus on and what they need to do, and this is a normal, necessary process at this age, but what is different today is that there are these new ways to become involved in stimuli that may not be helpful . . . and could be harmful.

Unit 2: Development Through Life
CD2
TR09 ## Chapter 4: Adulthood

Getting Started: Recording numbers, page 66

Interviewer: Listen as I ask eight friends of mine what age they think is the best age to be. Complete the information in the chart as you listen. Bruce, how old are you?

Bruce: Twenty-eight.

Interviewer: Twenty-eight. OK, well, I wanted to ask you, whaddya think is the best age? The best period in life?

Bruce: For me, it's these years – late twenties, I think.

Interviewer: Yeah? Late twenties?

Bruce: Yeah.

Interviewer: Julie, may I ask how old you are?

Julie: I'm twenty-five.

Interviewer: Twenty-five? OK. And may I ask what you think the best time of life is, for you, in your opinion?

Julie: Um, I, I think the best time of life is when you're a little child.

Interviewer: Oh!

Julie: The ages four through eight or so, eight or nine.

Interviewer: Huh.

Interviewer: Ann, can you tell me how old you are?

Ann: I sure can – I'm 57. I always have to stop and think.

Interviewer: Fifty-seven. OK. Well, what I wanted to ask you about today was what do you think is the best time of life? The best age to be?

Ann: Oh, the best age to be? Oh wow, that's a great question. Definitely not a teenager. I think the worst time, if you'd asked me that, was 12, 13, 14, 15. I think that's the most difficult time. The best time, I think, is probably, maybe in your thirties?

Interviewer: David, may I ask how old you are?

David: Forty-uh, almost 46.

Interviewer: And the, uh, the question I wanna ask you is whaddya think is the best age to be? Or, do you have an age that stands out in your mind as the best age?

David: Well, uh, physically, I'd like to be, oh, uh, somewhere in my twenties, but mentally, I think I would probably have to say I'm happy to be the age that I am.

Interviewer: Otis, can I ask you how old you are?

Otis: Seventy.

Interviewer: OK. And my question is, um, what do you think is the best period of your life? What, what's the best age to be? What, what was or what is or what will be?

Otis: Oh, golly, I have to think about that. The best period, well, uh, professionally, I, uh, I think the best for me was like, uh, 25 years ago, 30 years ago.

Interviewer: Gene, what's your age?

Gene: Uh, 71 last week.

Interviewer: OK, and Laurie, how old are you?

Laurie: I'm 68, 69 next month.

Interviewer: OK, and so, the question I want to ask is what do you think . . . what is the best age to be? How about you, Laurie?

Laurie: To be the age you are is the best age to be, so I love the age I am right now.

Interviewer: Well, were there any periods in your life that you enjoyed more than others?

Laurie: Um. Yes, my forties were wonderful.

Interviewer: And, Gene, how about you? What do you consider the best age to be, for yourself? The best period in your life?

Gene: Gee, I dunno.

Interviewer: Loleta, first I wanna ask you how old are you?

Loleta: I'm 77.

Interviewer: OK. Seventy-seven. And the question I wanna ask you is whaddya think is the best age to be? For you?

Loleta: Well, I look back at special times in my life and, oh, the period between graduation from college and getting married was wonderful for me.

Survey Part 1: The Best Age to Be
CD2
TR10 ### Responding to true/false statements, page 68

Interviewer: OK, Bruce, um, why is the late twenties better than, say, earlier twenties?

Bruce: Um, I think that when you're in your, in the early twenties, you're just getting over, um, teenage adolescent years, so now I think in the late twenties you kinda know a direction but, um, the early twenties are just too . . . you just kinda remember too many things of the teenage years, and you're still trying to get a plan. But in the twenties, late twenties, you kind of know what you wanna do, and you kind of have an idea of, of how to get it. And you know how to settle down, too. You can see a plan for getting things and also settling down.

Interviewer: Hmm. Um, is there a time in your life that you think you would call the most difficult time?

Bruce: Probably the teenage years, like 14, 15 –

Interviewer: Yeah?

Bruce: Sixteen.

Interviewer: The mid-teens.

Bruce: Yeah, I think the mid-teens were the worst.

Interviewer: So, Julie, why would you like to be a little girl again?

Julie: Um, I think, uh, I think lately because the age I'm at now, I feel is kind of a stressful age.

Interviewer: Huh.

Julie: When you're, when you're younger, you don't have as many worries and responsibilities.

Interviewer: Yeah.

Julie: You don't have all the stresses of life as an adult. I think at the age I'm at now, when you get out of college and you need to find a job –

Interviewer: Uh-huh.

Julie: And I'm single and I can't depend on my parents anymore –

Interviewer: Uh-huh.

Julie: And I have new responsibilities – just trying to get used to having new responsibilities – and also figure out what I wanna do – there's lots of decisions.

Interviewer: Uh-huh.

Julie: I don't always know what the best thing to do is. Um, those are things that I need to learn.

Interviewer: Yeah.

Julie: Yeah!

Interviewer: So, Ann, why was being in your thirties good?

Ann: Because in your thirties, you pretty much know what you like and what you don't like, and you're kind of settled into life. And, at least for me, that was a really good time. Actually, now that my sons are married and, and they're independent –

Interviewer: Uh-huh.

Ann: When I come to come to think about it, I probably do more interesting things now for myself than I did when I was in my thirties.

Interviewer: Huh! For example –

Ann: Well, now I'm playing in an orchestra, which I would never've had time to do when, when the boys were little and, um, and I, uh, read a lot more than I did.

Interviewer: Do you and your husband go out more?

Ann: Ha! We do! We do! We go out to movies, and we go out to dinner, and we hope to be able to travel!

 Survey Part 2: The Best Age to Be

CD2
TR11 **Summarizing what you have heard,** page 69

Interviewer: So, Otis, uh, professionally your early forties were your best time, you say?

Otis: Yeah. Well, actually, I would say maybe from, um, thirty-five to about fifty.

Interviewer: Why was that?

Otis: Um, I was much more receptive to new ideas, I lectured better, I read a lot more, and I was very interested in doing certain things in a different way.

Interviewer: Uh-huh.

Otis: Because when I was fifty, actually, is when I created about four courses that had never been taught at the university here before. I'd just come to the university, and I created all those courses and taught them regularly, and most of them worked.

Interviewer: That's great.

Otis: But I think in terms of feeling mature and responsible and, um, sensitive to the world around me, I think the last ten years have been the best.

Interviewer: OK.

Interviewer: So, what was so wonderful about your forties, Laurie?

Laurie: Well, 'cuz, well, I had, I had basically educated myself 'cuz I got my master's degree during my forties, and that was a very exciting time – I really enjoyed that a lot. And, um, my children had grown up, so I was beginning to feel free of a lot of my responsibilities and commitments, and I could focus on my own work, which is painting. And I also started studying music, which was really great 'cuz I hadn't done that before. And I met some wonderful people. It was a beginning.

Interviewer: So, Gene, you say you don't know what age is best, but is there any period in your life that you really loved more than others or –

Gene: The older, the older I get, the more I think about when I was younger but uh, but that's probably . . . I think the older you get, the more you think about your youth.

Interviewer: And the more –

Gene: At least when you get past a certain age.

Interviewer: Yeah, and the more you value it? The more you miss it?

Gene: Yeah. You know, when you're younger, you can't wait to grow up. And when you're old, you think, "What an idiot I was, and I should've understood that there were, that there were things that weren't quite so bad then," y'know. But you don't know when you're younger. For instance, you get up and you feel terrific, y'know, and you just take it for granted. But when you're older, and you wake up, I mean, you don't feel so well, y'know. I mean, you gotta, your bones hurt, and your joints hurt, and you gotta kind of, um, well, it takes a mental effort to get . . . and sometimes it takes like, uh, Laurie and I always talk about how long it takes to get going in the morning, y'know. In the army, we used to get up and ten minutes later we were out on the parade field. And now when we get up we gotta do our exercises. Then we gotta do our walk. Then we gotta do our bath. I mean, [laughing] it's like our job now. We don't have time to work anymore.

 Survey: The Best Age to Be

CD2
TR12 **Uses of get,** page 69

1.

Bruce: Um, I think that when you're in your, in the early twenties, you're just getting over, um, teenage adolescent years.

2.

Bruce: You can see a plan for getting things and also settling down.

3.

Julie: . . . when you get out of college and you need to find a job . . .

4.

Julie: . . . just trying to get used to having new responsibilities –

5.

Gene: I think the older you get, the more you think about your youth.

6.

Gene: For instance, you get up and you feel terrific . . .

7.

Gene: Laurie and I always talk about how long it takes to get going in the morning . . .

 Lecture: Anthony Brown, "Developmental Tasks of Early Adulthood"

CD2
TR13 **Before the Lecture: Paying attention to signal words,** page 74

1. By developmental tasks, I mean life changes that a person must accomplish as he or she grows and develops

2. Ideally, what's considered optimal at this point is for the young adult to be capable of supporting him- or herself completely – that includes financially, emotionally, and socially.

3. One of the major tasks for young adults is the development of a new and different type of relationship with parents – that is, one based on mutual adulthood.

4. the current economic climate in the world has made that much more difficult to achieve, and the result is that we see a lot more young adults living with their parents.

5. So, as I said, it, it can be difficult for young adult children to establish financial independence from their parents.

6. Of course, separation is the natural thing for adult children to do at this point – to leave their parents and, and start their own, uh, lives. But even though it's natural, this is still a crisis point in a family, when a child leaves.

7. So, we've talked about two of the important tasks of young adulthood.

 Lecture Part 1: "Separation from Parents"

 Listening for specific information, page 76

CD2
TR14 I'm going to speak about two of the major developmental tasks of young adulthood, and by developmental tasks, I mean life changes that a person must accomplish as he or she grows and develops. The young adult is in his or her early to mid-twenties, and at least in Western culture, um, this is the time for the achievement of independence from parents. Ideally, what's considered optimal at this point is for the young adult to be capable of supporting him- or herself completely – that includes financially, emotionally, and socially. [*slight pause*] OK, so we could say that one of the major tasks for young adults is the development of a new and different type of relationship with parents – that is, one based on mutual adulthood. Now, this is the sort of culmination of a long process of separation that starts in early childhood, and ideally in young adulthood, and the child physically separates and goes his or her own way in the world. Interestingly enough, this is a change that is happening later in, in life, in today's world, partly because it depends on the child's ability to become financially independent, and the current economic climate in the world has made that much more difficult to achieve, and the result is that we see a lot more young adults living with their parents, well, well into their twenties. So, as I said, it, it can be difficult for young adult children to establish financial independence from their parents. And then, establishing emotional independence can also be a difficult process, and not all children separate from their parents with equal success. Some children may never be successful at this, uh, they may be forever in the role of child and the parent forever in the role of parent. Of course, [*slight pause*] separation is the natural thing for adult children to do at this point – to leave their parents and, and start their own, uh, lives. But even though it's natural, this is still a crisis point in a family, when a child leaves, and some families don't handle it well. Change is a frightening thing for, for many people, but there's no escaping it. We all have to learn how to change throughout our lives.

 Lecture Part 2: "The Crisis of Intimacy versus
 Isolation"

CD2
TR15 **Listening for specific information,** page 78

And then there's a second task of young adulthood, which ties – uhh – into this whole business of getting married. Erik Erikson identifies, th, the period of young adulthood as the time when the young adult faces the crisis of intimacy versus isolation.

Well, the theory is that in adolescence, the child has developed a healthy uh ego identity, and of course in reality, um, for a variety of reasons, many people fail to develop this healthy identity in adolescence, but again, ideally, then, in young adulthood, this identity is ready and able to be joined with another, uh, traditionally in marriage. This involves the ability to make a commitment to someone, in, a, a close intimate way. Now, according to Erikson, healthy people during this period – umm – are able to compromise, to sacrifice, to negotiate – all of which one must do to make a marriage successful. This, then, as I said, is a second major development task, I mean, developmental task of this period. The ability to adapt to another person in this way will increase intimacy, or closeness and, and connection. Um, if this isn't achieved, the result is isolation, or in other words, a kind of avoiding of being in the world. Other people experience this as self-absorption, and we've seen, for example, um, someone who is a really accomplished research chemist, but they spend all their time in the lab, and their family is estranged. And, and, and, and this isn't a natural choice for a human being. We are built to be in groups, and people who isolate themselves often have, um, excellent reasons for doing so, but the reasons are negative . . . so, there is a fear of losing themselves or, or, being hurt if, if, they open up and are vulnerable to other people. So, there you have intimacy or isolation, and the challenge for the young adult is to resolve that crisis, and, as I said, success depends on the young adult having developed a healthy, a solid, healthy identity in adolescence. It's difficult to give yourself to another person in a relationship, if you do not have a self to give, if your self is not defined, if it is not solid . . . and, it puts great emotional stress on a relationship when two people are trying to deal with the developmental tasks of marriage, wh – wh –when they haven't yet dealt with the important developmental task involved in just being a separate person. That, ideally, should come first. And that brings me to an interesting point about marriage today . . . a, and that is that increasingly, in the West, people who in the past might have felt pressure to marry in their early twenties, uh, right out of college, now tend to stay single for a longer period of time. With this is the freedom, for example, to take more risks, to move to a different part of the country or to a different part of the world. And there is also, with, what with the divorce rate as high as it is, a certain reluctance, a skepticism about marriage as an institution. As a result, many young adults are waiting to get married until their late twenties or older. And in fact, the, the statistics show that couples who do wait till their late twenties to get married have a much lower divorce rate than, than those who marry in their early twenties. So, we've talked about two of the important tasks of young adulthood: the first, separation from parents, which involves, uh, renegotiating one's, one's relationship with parents; and the second, solving the crisis of intimacy versus isolation, that is, bringing a solid sense of one's self to a relationship with another person. And, the degree of success with which the young uh adult accomplishes these tasks will determine to a great extent their future success and satisfaction in life.

 **Unit 3: Nonverbal Messages**
CD2
TR16 **Chapter 5: Body Language**

Getting Started: Reading nonverbal cues, page 88

A. Hello!
B. Shhh. Quiet!
C. No! I am not interested.
D. I don't know. I have no idea.

E. Could you come here?
F. Good job!!
G. I am not telling the truth.
H. Wish me good luck!

Interview 1: Brazilian Body Language

CD2 TR17 **Responding to true/false statements,** page 90

Interviewer: Marcos, how many years have you lived in the United States?

Marcos: Ah, I was a student here for about five years, and then I, uh, went back and lived in Brazil for a while, and then I moved back eight years ago.

Interviewer: OK, and what I wanted to pick your brain about was, um, body language and things that you might remember noticing when you came here – things that North Americans do differently from people in Brazil, um, for example, eye contact. Is that something you noticed?

Marcos: Um, well, you know, there is a big difference. I've learned that North Americans are much more . . . How can I say this? It's very important for them to have, uh, your eye contact so that they know that you're with them in the conversation, that you're paying attention, and so forth. And what I've noticed about myself is that my eyes tend to, uh, wander in the distance and go to other places, and I've had people think that I wasn't paying attention –

Interviewer: Yeah?

Marcos: But I was just trying to focus.

Interviewer: Trying to focus. That's interesting. Uh, what about hand movements? Have you noticed a difference between Brazilians and Americans?

Marcos: Well, that's an interesting story. A part of my family in Brazil – well, these are people who were part of my first wife's family – and they were from Italy –

Interviewer: Uh-huh.

Marcos: And, uh, they talked with their hands a lot, and we had always noticed it, y'know, but we never thought that we did the same thing, uh, as Brazilians.

Interviewer: Oh!

Marcos: But on observing, uh, how seldom, uh, people here seem to make gestures, I've become more aware of the fact that Brazilians do indeed talk a lot with their hands.

Interviewer: Uh-huh! Well, what about the kinds of gestures we use, I mean, to signal certain things. Have you ever completely misunderstood a situation because of an unfamiliar gesture?

Marcos: Well, y'know, a case comes to mind. This was when my wife and I were living in Brazil, and we –

Interviewer: Now, your wife's North American, is that right?

Marcos: Yes, she is. And we were at a party one day at school, and we were standing quite, uh, far apart from each other, and she put out her right arm and started opening and closing her fing-, hand, and in Brazil, that, what that means is "Come closer." So I kept coming closer, and she turned around and walked away, and I was very confused. And later I asked her, "Why did you keep calling me if you didn't want to talk to me?" And she said, "I wasn't doing any such thing!"

Interviewer: Ha!

Marcos: So I repeated the gesture to her and what she meant to do was, was kind of wave at me, but that's not the way Brazilians wave. But it must've been very funny to the students that were watching because I kept walking towards her, and she kept walking away.

Interview 2: South Korean Body Language

CD2 TR18 **Responding to true/false statements,** page 91

Interviewer: SunRan, let me just ask, first of all, how long have you been in the United States?

SunRan: Ten years.

Interviewer: Ten years. OK, well, uh, can I ask you, are there any American hand signals that gave you trouble when you first came to the United States?

SunRan: Well, yeah! The way you say "come . . ." we do that kind of hand signal for a dog, not for people.

Interviewer: Oh! With your palm upward? That's for calling dogs in Korea?

SunRan: Yeah.

Interviewer: That must be shocking for Koreans who come here. Uh, what about eye contact? Is that different in Korea? Is it, is it OK for people to look at each other directly?

SunRan: Well, not a higher-level person. I mean, if I talk to my boss or to an older person, I should look at his mouth or chin, not in his eyes.

Interviewer: Really!

SunRan: And boys and girls – if they look in each other's eyes, it means they are interested.

Interviewer: Oh! So you shouldn't look directly at someone if you're not interested!

SunRan: No. But . . . I've been in the U.S. for 10 years and I think maybe Korea has changed a little this way.

Interviewer: How so?

SunRan: I think boys and girls in Korea use more eye contact now. Before, boys and girls went to different schools, but now they can go to the same schools . . .

Interviewer: So they have much more contact with each other?

SunRan: Yes.

Interviewer: I see. What are some other differences in body language between Korea and the U.S. . . . that you've noticed?

SunRan: Um, I find Americans tend to make a lot of facial expressions when they talk.

Interviewer: Oh.

SunRan: I think Koreans use less body language when they communicate.

Interviewer: Oh.

SunRan: It's considered more polite to stand still, sit still, try not to move anything.

Interviewer: That's true for men and women?

SunRan: That's both men and women.

Interviewer: Well –

Interviewer: In the past in Korea, when you moved your body a lot, like crossing your legs or crossing your arms, it was kind of a sign of, um, bad manners.

Interviewer: Well, that's interesting. Now you've been here for 10 years. Have you changed? Do you use your arms more now than . . . when you're talking? Or your hands?

SunRan: I use my arms and hands a lot – a lot of body language. Yes, I do.

Interviewer: More than, than you would if you were speaking Korean?

SunRan: Right. I . . . think it is changing a little now, so Korean people use more body language. But older Koreans still have this idea, so when I visit Korea, especially when I talk to my older relatives, I try to minimize that.

Interviewer: Are you able to do that?

SunRan: Not so well! [*laughs*] They always say, "How come you move so much? How come you don't sit still?"

 Interview 3: Japanese Body Language

CD2 TR19 **Restating what you have heard,** page 92

Interviewer: Airi, let's see, how long have you been here?

Airi: Twelve years.

Interviewer: OK, and you came here with your husband, who's American.

Airi: Yes, he's American.

Interviewer: So, I just, I wanted to ask you if you've ever had any misunderstandings because of differences in gestures that Americans use, or maybe eye contact, or –

Airi: Ah! Yes. I had an experience like that just after I came here . . . I, uh, participated in my husband's sister's – my sister-in-law's wedding . . .

Interviewer: Uh-huh?

Airi: . . . and after the ceremony, we took a family picture –

Interviewer: Uh-huh?

Airi: Like a, like a formal portrait. This is it.

Interviewer: Oh! You have it here!

Airi: Uh, like everyone is smiling with, uh, open mouths.

Interviewer: Yeah! Teeth showing!

Airi: Yeah, except me. And when I saw this picture, I felt really embarrassed.

Interviewer: Huh!

Airi: My husband's mother asked me, "Why didn't you smile?" So I said to her, uh, "I did smile!" The Japanese way.

Interviewer: Oh! So that's a cultural difference.

Airi: Yeah. In Japan, in this situation, like a formal portrait?

Interviewer: Uh-huh.

Airi: We usually just make a smile with our mouth, but we don't open our mouth.

Interviewer: Hmm! I was also wondering about eye contact. I've heard that too much eye contact in Japan is a bad thing. Is that true?

Airi: Well, I, I don't think . . . no, it's not bad . . . I think it's good in Japan also – good to look at each other.

Interviewer: Oh!

Airi: Like you're really listening to the person, really trying to understand.

Interviewer: Are there any differences in eye contact that you've noticed between Japan and the U.S.?

Airi: No, I think it's almost the same.

Interviewer: What about other differences that you've noticed?

Airi: Well, Americans use more, like, body language, like, uh – hand signals when they talk.

Interviewer: So gestures –

Airi: Yes, and they use different gestures. Like this gesture for "so-so, sort of," we don't have that in Japan.

Interviewer: Hmm!

Airi: Yeah.

Interviewer: So the gestures are different but there are also more of them.

Airi: That's right.

Interviewer: Now, you have been here for awhile, and also, your husband is American . . .

Airi: Yeah. [*laughs*] so I think I use my hands a lot.

Interviewer: More than typical?

Airi: Yeah, especially when I first started dating my husband, and we couldn't communicate very well – so I really wanted him to try to understand –

Interviewer: Yeah!

Airi: So I used my hands all the time.

Interviewer: You used everything you could! [*laughs*]

Airi: [*laughs*] It was like, "Please, please understand me!!"

 Determining which way this or that is pointing,

CD2 TR20 page 93

1.

Marcos: . . . there is a big difference. I've learned that North Americans are much more . . . How can I say this? It's very important for them to have, uh, your eye contact.

2.

Interviewer: You were trying to focus. That's interesting. Uh, what about hand movements?

3.

Interviewer: Have you noticed a difference between Brazilians and Americans?

Marcos: Well, that's an interesting story. A part of my family in Brazil . . . they were from Italy . . .

4.

Interviewer: Now, your wife's North American, is that right?

5.

Marcos: . . . she put out her right arm and started opening and closing her hand, and in Brazil, what that means is "Come closer."

 In Your Own Voice: Using your body to

CD2 TR21 **communicate,** page 96

Airi: I think I use my hands a lot.

Interviewer: More than typical?

Airi: Yeah, especially when I first started dating my husband, and we couldn't communicate very well – so I really wanted him to try to understand –

Interviewer: Yeah!

Airi: So I used my hands all the time.

Interviewer: You used everything you could! [*laughs*]

Airi: [*laughs*] It was like, "Please, please understand me!!"

Lecture: Ellen Summerfield, "Body Language Across Cultures"

CD2 TR22 **Before the Lecture: Mapping,** page 98

Maybe we should begin by mentioning an obvious one; that's what we call body language, that is, what we are saying by our posture, the way in which we hold ourselves, our gestures, that is, use of our hands; our facial expressions – all the things that say something to the other person, not through words, but simply how we present ourselves, how we move. Let's see, our eye contact, for example, is one that we may not think of right away, but, it's extremely important, and our tone of voice. How about the meaning of touch? Touch communication, that is, who has permission to touch whom and under what circumstances.

Lecture Part 1: "Aspects of Body Language"

Mapping, page 99

CD2
TR23 OK. Today we're going to begin our discussion of nonverbal communication. Now, experts in the field of communication estimate that somewhere between 60 and 90 percent of everything we communicate is nonverbal. How can that possibly be true? After all, we put so much emphasis on our words when we're trying to communicate something. We think about what we want to say, we worry about what we didn't say. We think about what we should have said. I mean, we're concerned about how the other person interprets our words, and we interpret the other person's words. So, there's enormous emphasis in all our interactions on words. What about this 60 to 90 percent that is supposedly nonverbal? What does that mean exactly? OK. Let me ask you to think about some of the ways in which you communicate nonverbally – just the broad areas. Maybe we should begin by mentioning an obvious one; that's what we call body language, that is, what we are saying by our posture, the way in which we hold ourselves, our gestures, that is, use of our hands; our facial expressions – all the things that say something to the other person, not through words, but simply how we present ourselves, how we move. Let's see, our eye contact, for example, is one that we may not think of right away, but, it's extremely important, and our tone of voice. How about the meaning of touch? Touch communication, that is, who has permission to touch whom and under what circumstances. A very important point that I'd like to make is that nonverbal communication is difficult enough to study and understand in one's own culture, but – it becomes extremely complicated when we are trying to understand how nonverbal communication functions in another culture, that is, one we're unfamiliar with. I mean, after all, if we're learning about another culture and learning the language of that culture, another language, what do we learn but words – the meaning of words and how they fit together and the pronunciation of words. So that, when we learn French, we can take our dictionary and look up fromage, or when we learn German, we can find out what Käse is. But, there's no dictionary of nonverbal communication. So, where do we find out what a certain toss of a head means? Or a certain blink of the eye? Or the physical distance between people? It's very easy to misinterpret these cues or to miss them altogether. If you're puzzled by what's happening to you in a foreign culture, it's probably the nonverbals that are causing the communication problem.

Lecture Part 2: "Cross-Cultural Misunderstandings"

CD2
TR24 **Mapping,** page 100

So, the nonverbals are probably responsible for most cross-cultural confusion. Let's see, let me give you one or two examples of how this can happen. A simple one is with eye contact. Americans tend to think that looking directly into another person's eye is appropriate, and that if you look away or you look down, you may be avoiding responsibility, or showing disrespect. And this is considered to be negative. We learn to "look me straight in the eye!" Look me straight in the eye. Now in some other cultures, it's a sign of disrespect to look at another person straight in the eye. In Japan, for example, there's much less eye contact than in the United States. So . . . something as simple as that can cause great confusion. To give another cross-cultural example from Japan, I can tell you that when I first began working in Japan, I was, oh boy, I was awfully confused because I was paying attention to what was said to me rather than to the nonverbal cues. We have a study-abroad program and when I was dealing with my Japanese colleagues, I would often ask questions, you know, that had to do with the program for our students. And I would ask one particular colleague if we could make certain changes. Now, I have great respect for this colleague, and I know that he wanted to cooperate. There were times when I would ask him things like, for instance, "Can we allow students in the dormitory to stay out later at night?" And often the response I would get verbally was that maybe we could do that, and I always interpreted this as a green light, as a strong possibility, because maybe for me verbally means "Maybe! Yes! Probably! Let's find a way!" After all, he hadn't said "no." What I didn't understand was that for my colleague, who didn't want to embarrass me by saying, saying, speaking the word "no" directly – which would be considered impolite in his culture – he was telling me "no" by saying "maybe" and giving me other cues with his body language, and I had to learn to recognize what those cues were. Well, can you imagine what they might be, for example? Well, I started to realize that it had to do with how he said maybe, it had to do with his tone: whether he said, "Well, maybe!" meaning "Maybe, yes!" or "Maybe," meaning "maybe not." It had to do, perhaps, whether he looked embarrassed, or whether he looked uncomfortable when he said that, or whether he seemed excited about the idea, or not. Or, or maybe how he, his posture, his body posture, how he held himself. I had to start observing those things. Now, I'll admit to you that it's still very difficult for me because I don't understand the nonverbal cues in Japanese society as well as I might understand them here in my own culture. But now I'm much more aware that I have to pay attention to them and that I have to learn to observe them more carefully. And you know what? That's probably the most important lesson of nonverbal communication – that is, we have to pay attention, to observe closely, what is happening both in our own patterns of communication and in those of the people around us, and that this really deserves our study and our attention. I mean, it's not only extremely interesting, but it's so important if we want to understand the more hidden sides of communication.

Unit 3: Nonverbal Messages
CD3
TR01 ## Chapter 6: Touch, Space, and Culture

Getting Started: Recording information, Step B, page 103

Social distance varies depending on the situation. Research has identified four different zones – or distances – that are common for North Americans. For each zone, there is a wide range, depending on personality. The first zone is the public zone, which is usually more than 12 feet, or 3.6 meters. This is the distance we like to keep between ourselves and other people when we are walking, for example. Of course, in a crowded city, this isn't possible. The second zone is the business/social zone, which averages 6 feet, or approximately 1.8 meters. This is a good distance for talking in a public place with people we don't know well, for example, in an office. The third zone is the personal zone, which averages 1 foot 6 inches, or 46 centimeters. This is a comfortable distance for North Americans having a conversation with a friend. The closest zone is the intimate zone – less than 18 inches or 50 centimeters. This zone is for romantic partners, but it can also be used as a way to threaten a person, to say, "I am stronger than you, and I can attack you."

Recording information, Step C, page 103

CD3
TR02 Social distance also varies depending on one's culture. The following averages for the personal zone have been identified for North America, Western Europe, Japan, and the Middle East. The average North American is comfortable with a personal distance of about 46 centimeters, while in Western Europe, the comfort zone for personal interactions ranges from 36 to 41 centimeters. Japanese prefer a much greater distance, approximately 91 centimeters. In contrast, personal distance in the Middle East is much closer – approximately 20 to 30 centimeters.

Interview 1: Marcos: Touch and Space

CD3
TR03 **Summarizing what you have heard, page 106**

Interviewer: Marcos, do Brazilians stand close together when they're talking?

Marcos: Oh, much closer than North Americans, yeah. Yeah, I've had several interesting cross-cultural experiences with this, uh, one time I was in a classroom, I was talking to a student of mine about some assignment – it was after class and I kept – um, he was a gentleman from Korea – and I kept getting closer to him, and he kept backing up.

Interviewer: [*short laugh*] Oh, dear.

Marcos: And I didn't really realize what was going on until I saw this, this look of total despair on his face, and I realized that he had backed up the whole length of the classroom, and now we were in one corner of the room.

Interviewer: Really?

Marcos: He looked very uncomfortable, and I had obviously, uh, invaded his body bubble, his space.

Interviewer: Yeah! Huh. How about touch? Do Brazilians touch each other more than North Americans?

Marcos: Yes, in Brazil, it's really common for people who are talking to you to stand really close and to touch you often, or to put their arm around you, or something, depending on who it is.

Interviewer: Now this is touching between male and female?

Marcos: Uh, let's see, uh, yes, male/female, uh, but I also think it's not uncommon for male friends to, uh, touch each other, say, to put an arm around the shoulder or something.

Interviewer: Uh-huh. Do you find, have you found that you've modified your bubble, your space, to accommodate us "cold North Americans"? Do you stand farther away from people now? And maybe not touch people as much?

Marcos: Yes, and I, uh, think it's a partly unconscious process – you just modify. I mean, if you don't, then, uh, when you're standing in line, you get too close to people, uh, and then, uh, they turn around, and they stare.

Interviewer: Yeah.

Marcos: So, uh, yeah, I feel that I have had to enlarge my bubble –

Interviewer: Yeah.

Marcos: And, and stand, uh, a little farther, uh, than I would. And, I've noticed in my family, too, you know, I've noticed that when we lived in Brazil, we were much more, uh, physical, or walked more closely or touched more often in public, than we do here.

Interviewer: Interesting.

Marcos: I think especially between my wife and me this has happened because it's when one looks around, and there aren't very many people touching each other in public, then one feels a little self-conscious.

Interview 2: SunRan: Touch and Space

CD3
TR04 **Summarizing what you have heard, page 107**

Interviewer: SunRan, have you noticed big differences in how people touch in the U.S.?

SunRan: Well, one big difference is shaking hands. Men and women in Korea don't usually shake hands, so I had to learn to do that when I came here.

Interviewer: Uh-huh.

SunRan: So the first time I went back to visit Korea, I forgot, and I tried to shake hands, and they don't do that. So I was . . . kind of embarrassed.

Interviewer: Do people in Korea touch at all in public?

SunRan: Well, in Korea we kinda tend to show more affection to the same sex than the opposite sex – so, as friends, not as a partner.

Interviewer: I see.

SunRan: So, like, if I have a girlfriend, it's normal to walk around hand-in-hand or arm-in-arm.

Interviewer: Uh-huh?

SunRan: Yeah, I did that a lot in Korea, but I can't do it here, in the U.S.

Interviewer: Uh-huh.

SunRan: And here, men and women show a lot more affection than in Korea.

Interviewer: Men and women?

SunRan: Yeah.

Interviewer: Is it wrong in Korea for a man and woman to touch each other in public?

SunRan: You're not supposed to!

Interviewer: Ah, interesting. Even if they're married?

SunRan: Yeah. You know, the first thing that kinda came as a real shock to me when I arrived here was kids, high school kids – they hug and kiss at school. That was a real shock to me.

Interviewer: Hmm!

SunRan: And little boys and girls – they have their first kiss when they're . . . like . . . six or seven. That's strange, too, because we never, never did anything like that until, until we were older, maybe twenties.

Interviewer: Hmm. Now, SunRan, you've been here for about 10 years, right?

SunRan: Yes.

Interviewer: And you've been back to Korea recently, haven't you? Do you think anything has changed?

SunRan: Yes, I was in Korea last year, and . . . yeah, it is a little bit different now from when I lived there. Uh, for example, I think people shake hands more now . . .

Interviewer: Hmm . . .

SunRan: . . . but it's still not very common for a man and a woman to shake hands.

Interviewer: Any other differences that you noticed on your last visit?

SunRan: Well, yes, I was in Seoul, and I saw some young couples on the street . . . uh, touching or holding hands.

Interviewer: Hugging?

SunRan: Uh, I didn't see hugging, just touching – so maybe in the big city it's different now from . . . from before.

Interview 3: Airi: Touch

CD3 TR05 **Summarizing what you have heard, page 108**

Interviewer: Airi, what about differences that you might have noticed in space or in how Americans touch each other?

Airi: Yeah, I think many Japanese, uh, have the same opinion about hugging.

Interviewer: Yeah?

Airi: Hugging and kissing. In Japan, at the beginning of our relationship, . . . my husband?

Interviewer: Yeah?

Airi: He was confused because my family would never hug him, much less kiss him.

Interviewer: Huh.

Airi: Yeah, my mother never, never touched him or, you know, so he worried, "Maybe she doesn't love me."

Interviewer: Interesting!

Airi: Yeah, and also, uh, he couldn't communicate with her very well. So, so he felt really confused and nervous.

Interviewer: Yeah, 'cuz in the U.S., you know, if you can't talk, you can at least put your arm on someone to show them –

Airi: Yeah! Show love –

Interviewer: Communicate that way. Huh. So, you say your parents didn't hug or kiss him. Did they hug or kiss you? I mean, within your family, do, in Japan, do people hug each other? Like, did your mother hug you?

Airi: No, I think never! When I was a child, maybe she did –

Interviewer: Yeah?

Airi: But . . . no, not after that. We just communicated by words. Sometimes we shake hands, but never hug.

Interviewer: Huh.

Airi: Now I can understand how my husband felt.

Interviewer: Yeah?

Airi: Yeah, since I came here, I've come to understand his feelings because my American family always hugs – they hug and kiss – and at first I felt really, really confused . . . but little by little, I began to feel more love and affection for them.

Interviewer: Uh-huh . . .

Airi: I started to feel really comfortable with that.

Interviewer: So, it's really rubbed off on you? You enjoy hugging?

Airi: Yeah, yeah! I really like it!! You know, I had a funny experience recently . . .

Interviewer: Yeah?

Airi: I have a good friend in Japan. I was just back in Japan last month, and I was so happy to see her that I opened my arms like . . . like . . .

Interviewer: To give her a hug?

Airi: [*laughing*] Yes! I just forgot! And her face – her expression was . . . just . . . she was shocked! And afraid, so . . . [*laughing*]

Interviewer: That's funny!

Airi: Yeah – so I didn't hug her. But . . . she was just accepted to nursing school in Japan, so I wrote, and I told her that when she graduates, I am going to give her a big hug!! And she wrote back: "Airi, I am . . . looking forward . . . to your hug!" [*both laugh*]

 Decoding the meaning of word stress, page 109

CD3 TR06 **1.**

Marcos: He looked very uncomfortable, and I had obviously, uh, invaded his body bubble, his space.

Interviewer: Yeah! Huh. How about touch? Do Brazilians touch each other more than North Americans?

2.

Interviewer: Now this is touching between male and female?

Marcos: Uh, let's see, uh, yes, male/female, uh, but I also think it's not uncommon for male friends to, uh, touch each other, say, to put an arm around the shoulder or something.

3.

SunRan: And little boys and girls – they have their first kiss when they're . . . like . . . six or seven. That's strange, too, because we never, never did anything like that until, until we were older.

4.

Interviewer: Huh. So, you say your parents didn't hug or kiss him. Did they hug or kiss you?

5.

Airi: No, I think never! When I was a child, maybe she did –

6.

Airi: Now I can understand how my husband felt.

Interviewer: Yeah?

Airi: Yeah, since I came here, I've come to understand his feelings . . .

7.

Airi: [*laughing*] And her face – her expression was . . . just . . . she was shocked!

In Your Own Voice: Using comparison/contrast,

CD3 TR07 **page 112**

Marcos. 1.

Interviewer: Are there things that North Americans do differently from people in Brazil, um, for example, eye contact. Is that something you noticed?

Marcos: Um, well, you know, there is a big difference.

2.

Marcos: . . . that's not the way Brazilians wave.

3.

Interviewer: Marcos, do Brazilians stand close together when they're talking?

Marcos: Oh, much closer than North Americans.

SunRan. 1.

SunRan: Um, I find Americans tend to make a lot of facial expressions when they talk.

2.

SunRan: I think Koreans use less body language when they communicate.

3.

SunRan: So, like, if I have a girlfriend, it's normal to walk around hand-in-hand or arm-in-arm. I did that a lot in Korea, but I can't do it here, in the U.S.

Airi. 1.

Interviewer: Are there any differences in eye contact that you've noticed between Japan and the U.S.?

Airi: No, I think it's almost the same.

2.

Airi: Americans use more, like, body language, like, uh – hand signals when they talk.

Interviewer: So gestures –

Airi: Yes, and they use different gestures. Like this gesture for "so-so, sort of" – we don't have that in Japan.

Interviewer: So the gestures are different but there are also more of them.

Airi: That's right.

Lecture: Mara Adelman, "Nonverbal Communication: The Hidden Dimension of Communication"

CD3
TR08

Before the Lecture: Listening for stress and intonation, page 114

1. How much of those expressions are conveyed through <u>verbal</u> communication? More often than not, our intense emotions are conveyed <u>nonverbally</u>.

2. More often than not, our intense emotions are conveyed nonverbally through <u>gestures, body position, facial expression, vocal cues, eye contact, use of space, and touching</u>.

3. Imagine what would happen if you don't understand this bubble. What might you experience? Possibly <u>discomfort, irritation</u>, maybe even <u>anger</u>.

4. It could express <u>affection, anger, playfulness, control, status</u>. . . . These are just a few functions of touch.

5. In <u>some</u> cultures, it is common to see same-sex friends holding hands and embracing in public. This behavior is not interpreted as sexual. However, think about this behavior in some <u>other</u> cultures. Is it appropriate?

Lecture Part 1: "Sarcasm and Proxemics"

Summarizing what you have heard, page 116

CD3
TR09

Today, we're going to start looking at nonverbal language. Nonverbal communication has often been referred to as the "hidden dimension" of communication. Sometimes this dimension is so subtle that we do not even recognize the ways it shapes what we're saying or how people interpret our meaning. In fact, when you think about it, think of some of the emotions that you express in everyday life, like happiness, joy, sadness, and anger, irritation. How much of those expressions are conveyed through <u>verbal</u> communication? More often than not, our intense emotions are conveyed <u>nonverbally</u> [*slight pause*] through <u>gestures, body position, facial expression, vocal cues, eye contact, use of space, and touching</u>. OK. Now, let me make two points about how nonverbal communication functions. One is, sometimes when we communicate, it may only be through the nonverbal cues. The nonverbal gesture carries all our meaning. But, secondly, nonverbal cues also function to help us interpret the verbal message, and this is the point I want to focus on first – that nonverbal cues help interpret, a verbal message. Where we see this really in a very subtle way is through the use of humor and sarcasm. Y'know, in humor and sarcasm, the verbal message – y'know, what is actually said – is only a small part of the message. It's often the nonverbal cues that signal: "Hey, how's this message to be taken, seriously or not? I mean, do they really mean it, or are they joking?" Take, for example, when an American sees a new style of clothing which they may not like – how they might signal that they don't like it. Well, they might say, "Oh, <u>that's</u> a good look." Well, OK, now, if you're from a different culture, how do you know if they really mean it, or if they're being sarcastic, and they really mean the opposite? Well, it's very difficult because it's the nonverbal cues – not the words – that are carrying the meaning here. It's usually the tone of voice or a facial expression. I guess this is why a lot of international students often tell me that it's humor that's the most difficult part of American culture to understand. And similarly, when Americans go abroad. There's another area of nonverbal communication that is often overlooked, and in this case, the nonverbal gesture carries all the meaning – and that is proxemics. That's P-R-O-X-E-M-I-C-S. Proxemics refers to our personal space. Y'know, the anthropologist Edward Hall calls this personal space of ours our "body bubbles." Body bubbles are interesting because they're very subtle. You hardly ever recognize them until someone pops your bubble. In other words, when somebody comes too close, or violates your private space, you are suddenly conscious – you become conscious of the bubble. So, what do you do when somebody pops your bubble? Do you feel uncomfortable? Do you move away? Do you turn your position? Do you put your books in front of you? Do you suddenly close your jacket? We always, we tend to adapt our body position when our bubbles get invaded. We see this in crowded elevators, for example. Body bubbles are influenced by many factors: How intimate is the relationship? What is the social context – a party or a bus? What is the gender relationship? However, a strong influence on body bubbles is culture. For example, in Latin American and Middle Eastern cultures, the kind of conversational space, the space between two people just engaged in everyday conversations, is relatively very close compared to Asian and American cultures. Imagine what would happen if you don't understand this bubble. What might you experience? Possibly <u>discomfort, irritation,</u> maybe even <u>anger</u>.

Lecture, Part Two: "Touch"

Summarizing what you have heard, page 117

CD3
TR10

And a third area of nonverbal communication, an area that's extremely powerful, where there are very strong norms – um, that's kind of social, unspoken social rules – strong norms that are easily violated is the area of touching. Touch is one of the most sensitive areas of nonverbal communication because touch is never neutral. Take the case of shaking hands with someone. We never think of shaking hands as a form of touch; it seems almost like a ritual. But, in fact, it's one of the major forms of touch between strangers. Now, in American culture, for example, we value firm handshakes. I mean, if the handshake is weak and limp, we might say, "He or she shakes hands like a fish." Touch is really amazing. It's very subtle and complex. Think for a moment about some of the functions of touch. What could it express? Well, it could express <u>affection, anger, playfulness, control, status</u>. . . . These are just a few functions of touch. Two major influences on touching behavior – think about your body bubbles again – one is gender, and the other is culture. We can see both influences – of gender and of culture – when we contrast same-sex touching – this'd be touching between two men or between two women. In <u>some</u> cultures, it is common to see same-sex friends holding hands and embracing in public. This behavior is not interpreted as sexual. However, think about this behavior in some <u>other</u> cultures. Is it appropriate? Could it be taboo? I recall my own surprise. I remember when I was visiting in China, and I would see young men holding hands in the streets, and young women, also. And at first, I was surprised, but I thought it was, y'know, very affectionate, very warm. So I decided that I was going to incorporate the same habit when I came back to the United States. So my sister and I started to hold hands in public. But we felt very awkward about it, and we stopped doing it. So you see the norms for touching are very powerful. They're easy to violate and, as I discovered, they're difficult to change. That is why it is very important to understand what is appropriate touch and what is taboo in another culture. Last, I think we have to remember that even misinterpretations and confusion in nonverbal communication don't always end in serious misinterpretations, or anger, or alienation. They're oftentimes the source of a lot of humor, a lot of laughter, and a lot of camaraderie between people of different cultures.

Unit 4: Interpersonal Relationships
Chapter 7: Friendship

Getting Started: Listening for specific information, page 128

Interviewer: Otis, can you tell me the name of one of your good friends?

Otis: Gee, that's difficult! I have so many good friends.

Interviewer: OK, tell me one.

Otis: OK, uh, Tom.

Interviewer: And when and where did you meet him?

Otis: Uh, at Yale in – I guess it was 1956. We were in the same class, and we had a lot of interests in common, like music, uh . . .

Interviewer: David, who is one of your best friends?

David: Uh, let's say Douglas.

Interviewer: And when and where did you meet him?

David: In college – we were both studying music.

Interviewer: And when was that?

David: Uh, let's see, 1982.

Interviewer: Pam, can you name a good friend of yours?

Pam: Uh, one of my best friends is Jeanette.

Interviewer: And when and how did you get to be friends?

Pam: Um, oh, back in 1981, I think, when we were in grade school. We were both social outcasts.

Interviewer: Yeah?

Pam: Yeah, we were both terrible at sports.

Interviewer: Tony, can you tell me the name of one of your best friends?

Tony: Uh, Hubert.

Interviewer: And how did you meet him?

Tony: We met in college. We were in classes together, and we just got to be good friends.

Interviewer: How long ago was this?

Tony: How long? Umm . . . Oh! Twenty-seven years!

Interviewer: Catherine, who would you say is one of your good friends?

Catherine: Uh, Odette.

Interviewer: OK, Odette. And when and where did you meet her?

Catherine: Uh, I met her in graduate school. And that was, let's see, 1999.

Interviewer: Ruth, who's one of your best friends?

Ruth: Oh! Well, the first person that comes to mind is Esther.

Interviewer: How did you get to be friends?

Ruth: Well, I met her in 1996 at my synagogue. I already knew about her from another friend, and when I met her, I just knew I wanted to be friends.

Interview Part 1: Starting Friendships
Retelling, page 130

Interviewer: Catherine, how long have you and I been . . . how long have we known each other?

Catherine: Let's see, we met when you interviewed me for a teaching job. Was it . . . seven, eight years ago?

Interviewer: Yeah, that's about right.

Catherine: But we began to be friends, um, I think it . . . what might've started it was when I asked you a favor, which was to help me give my cat, Sophie, a flea bath.

Interviewer: Oh, yes!

Catherine: Yeah. That was, that was hard for me. It was hard for me to ask that kind of favor of someone I didn't know that well 'cuz, you know, it seemed fairly bothersome, but it . . . it turned out to be kinda fun.

Interviewer: Yeah, it was fun! I still have the scars [*both laugh*]. . . . And after that, we started to be good friends. One thing that I've realized about you is that you have a lot of close friends from, you know, different periods in your life. How have your friendships gotten started?

Catherine: Hmm, well, I'd say that most of my friendships have sprung from some kind of shared interest, y'know, either at work or school or somewhere else. I have made a lot of friends at work. I value work a lot, and I feel like I have a particular work ethic, and so if I'm working with other people who have the same work ethic, that, for me, is, is something very large that we have in common, it makes for a, um, a good base for a possible friendship. Or, sometimes it's just that I have some, I don't know, some sense of "Yeah, this is a person that I'd like to get to know" because I heard them make a remark that I thought was funny or interesting.

Interviewer: You mentioned your friend Odette earlier. How did you two get to be friends?

Catherine: Oh! Well, let's see, um, I was going to graduate school, and I was taking a course in linguistics. And I noticed this other woman in the same class, and I really liked the way she looked, the way, y'know, and I remember thinking, "Oh, she's too cool! She would never wanna be friends with someone like me!" And I didn't talk to her 'cuz, I was just so intimidated by her coolness – oh gosh. And then, I think what happened, we were in a study group together and got a chance to talk. At some point, she revealed to me that she'd thought I was too cool for her, too. And we ended up being great friends. Yeah, and we realized that neither of us was that cool after all [*both laugh*].

Interview Part 2: Maintaining Friendships
Retelling, page 131

Interviewer: Catherine, you have quite a few long-distance friendships. How do you maintain them?

Catherine: Yeah, well, friendship is very important to me, um, I think friendships need tending. I, I put a big value on being current with my friends, and that's something that's hard to do long distance. But there are friends I have that I don't live close to that I have managed to stay very close to. My friend Odette lives back East, and we talk on the phone at least once a week, usually for an hour at a time, so I stay current with her, um, by talking.

Interviewer: So do you phone your other long-distance friends, too?

Catherine: Uh not so much. I use e-mail with some of my friends, but I actually still love to write letters and get letters . . .

Interviewer: So, snail mail . . .

Catherine: Yeah, and I have one friend – Doug – that I've been exchanging letters with for more than 20 years, and it's, it's a cool thing 'cuz, I still have all of them . . .

Interviewer: Wow!

Catherine: . . . and so . . . it's a concrete record of, um, you know, of what we've been doing all these years.

Interviewer: Huh!

Catherine: Yeah. We met when we were working at the same place. And then he went to Taiwan for two years and we wrote letters. We didn't know each other all that well, but we got to know each other through letters over the first two years, and ever since then, we've been good friends.

Interviewer: That's nice!

Catherine: Yeah, it's, it's cool.

Interviewer: So, telephone, snail mail, e-mail, what else?

Catherine: Skype! My old friend Corey in Chicago – we used to talk on the phone but now we Skype – he's actually the only friend I Skype with . . . and it's great because we'll be talking, and he'll say something like, "You actually don't look bad for your age" [*both laugh*]. And I recognize the room where he's sitting 'cuz, I've visited them, and his wife, Misayo, will walk through, and she'll stop and show me her knitting, and I'll show her what I'm working on – 'cause I've just started getting into knitting, and then his dog Peanut will wander through [*both laugh*] – and I've met Peanut, so it's like I've just dropped in on them for a visit.

 Interview Part 3: What Friends Do for Each Other
CD3 TR14 **Summarizing what you have heard,** page 131

Interviewer: So, in your view, what is it that good friends do for each other, Catherine?

Catherine: Well, I think friends . . . I feel like one thing I want my friends to do is to call me on things, you know, to let me know if I do something that upsets them for whatever reason. I think that's one thing friends, you know, do for each other, and that's why sometimes friendship can get prickly and hard. Um, and you can fight, but I've never, I've never felt fighting was bad. It's just showing that you care. But other things, I think friends, um, provide comfort and support and adventure and jokes! Especially with old friends. You share jokes that you've created together, that you've understood, and all you have to do is say one word, and the other person can go off into peals of laughter and that's, that's pretty, um –

Interviewer: It's powerful.

Catherine: Yeah, it is. And it's a great way to mark time, I think. To realize that you've actually accrued this common –

Interviewer: History!

Catherine: Yeah!

Interviewer: How about more recent friendships?

Catherine: Well, yeah, I should say my friendships have kind of shifted since my son Leo was born.

Interviewer: Yeah?

Catherine: I've made a number of good friends – being a parent is so all-consuming that it really bonds you with people who are going through the same experience.

Interviewer: Yeah!

Catherine: So these friendships have become more the day-to-day focus of friendship for me.

Interviewer: Huh.

Catherine: But I'm really happy for e-mail, and Skype, and the phone, and yeah – letters! . . . so I can keep up with the friends that I've known for so long, and have this great history with. . . . I think of friends as the family that we get to choose and that's, that's why friendship's such a wonderful thing.

 Interview Part 3: What Friends Do for Each Other
CD3 TR15 **Listening for verb tense and aspect,** page 132

1.

Catherine: . . . and I was taking a course in linguistics. And I noticed this other woman in the same class . . .

2.

Catherine: At some point, she revealed to me that she'd thought I was too cool for her, too. And we ended up being great friends.

3.

Catherine: . . . I have one friend – Doug – that I've been exchanging letters with for more than 20 years . . .

4.

Catherine: . . . his wife, Misayo, will walk through, and she'll stop and show me her knitting, and I'll show her what I'm working on . . .

5.

Catherine: Um, and you can fight, but I've never, I've never felt fighting was bad.

 In Your Own Voice: Describing a typical scene and
CD3 TR16 **activities,** page 134

Catherine: . . . and it's great because we'll be talking, and he'll say something like, "You actually don't look bad for your age" [*both laugh*]. And I recognize the room where he's sitting 'cuz, I've visited them, and his wife, Misayo, will walk through, and she'll stop and show me her knitting, and I'll show her what I'm working on – and . . . then his dog Peanut will wander through [*both laugh*] . . .

 Lecture: Kenneth Warden, "Looking at Friendship"
CD3 TR17 **Before the Lecture: Using morphology, context, and nonverbal cues to guess meaning,** page 137

1. But it's also rather subjective; friendship means very different things to different people.

2. As a therapist, I'm always thinking about a client's social network. Along with sleep patterns and appetite, this is an important indicator of a person's general functioning. When I work with a client who's suicidal, it's always critical to take into account that person's support systems, and, and by that, I'm talking about family and friends

3. You probably know of adults who consider themselves "loners" and say that they are content with that condition.

4. There can be a lot of pain involved with friendship – it's a risky business. When we make friends, or try to make them, we become vulnerable to rejection. Each of us probably has a painful childhood memory of being cast aside by one friend in favor of another.

5. . . . you may have heard of the concept of the "overscheduled child" – who is always busy, always going off to piano lessons or football practice or ballet class.

 Lecture Part 1: "The Role of Friendship in Good Mental Health"
CD3 TR18 **Listening for specific information,** page 139

In some respects, friendship seems like a very straightforward topic – everyone wants friends; most of us have friends. But it's also rather subjective; friendship means very different things to different people. What I'll be focusing on today is the importance of friendship to me, as an individual and as a psychotherapist, and then on some ways in which friendship is challenged today. My first memory of consciously contemplating friendship was as a young boy – I was about six or seven years old – and I heard an old song on the radio – "People." "People who need people are the luckiest people in the world." And I remember thinking: Is that really true? Do we need people? And is it OK to need people? And, as I've gotten older, more and more, I tend to answer that question in the affirmative. As a therapist, I'm always thinking about a client's social network. Along with sleep patterns and appetite, this is an important indicator of a person's general functioning. When I work with a client who's suicidal, it's always critical to take into account that person's support systems, and, and by that, I'm talking about family and friends. Does that person feel supported in the world? Do they have meaningful connections? There are two reasons why I think about that, and the first one is . . . the person who does feel supported is much less likely to attempt suicide in the first place. Suicide is very often the manifestation of an abject sense of alienation. And second, if a person is suicidal, it's very important to hook them up with their support systems so that they can be monitored and, and kept safe. Someone without friends is almost certain to be depressed. You probably know of adults who consider themselves "loners" and say that they are content with that condition. My sense is that while that may in part be true, it's almost always the function of a defense mechanism. There can be a lot of pain involved with friendship – it's a risky business. When we make friends, or try to make them, we become vulnerable to rejection. Each of us probably has a painful childhood memory of being cast aside by one friend in favor of another. And that really hurts. Rejection by friends is especially painful for children. So, many loners, after repeated rejection, adapt by consciously deciding not to get close to anyone. It's easier that way, and it's less painful. In effect, they're saying, "If I tell you who I am, and you don't like who I am, that's all I got. So I don't want to take that chance. I don't want to let you know who I really am." And of course, it's impossible to form a friendship if you're isolating yourself from other people like this. To make friends you have to run the risk of being rejected.

 Lecture Part 2: "New Challenges to Friendship"

 Listening for specific information, page 141

CD3 TR19 I want to talk about some of the challenges to . . . friendship that I see in modern life today. One has its roots in childhood, which of course is when we learn how to make friends. There's been a lot of study recently of how contemporary life affects children – you may have heard of the concept of the "overscheduled child" – who is always busy, always going off to piano lessons or football practice or ballet class. Of course, activities are good, but children also need unstructured time – in a safe place, of course – where they can just "hang out" with their peers – without tasks or deadlines. It is in those moments that a child can really get to know another child, and that is the basis of developing life-long friendships.

And of course, the pressures of modern life have an impact on adult friendships as well. Ask a friend today, "How are you?" and odds are the answer will be, "I'm so tired!" or "I'm much too busy!" or both. People spend more time at work, and the result is less quality time with family and friends. We may say that friendship is the most important thing in life, but that doesn't prevent us from moving across the country to take a better job if we have the opportunity.

Now this brings me to another aspect of modern life that may influence friendships – and one that I find extremely interesting and at the same time worrisome – and that has to do with the impact that social networking has had on . . . on the way in which people conduct their friendships. Facebook, instant messaging, texting, Twitter – these forms of communication are replacing to a great extent the kind of contact that friendships used to rely on – face-to-face interaction. Go to any café or

public place and it seems like almost everyone is "wired" – they're using some kind of electronic means of communication – even if they are sitting with a group of friends.

I mentioned earlier how mobility – for example, moving across the country for a new job – how that presents a huge challenge if we're trying to maintain a friendship, and in the past, it would probably have spelled the end of the friendship. Well, clearly, Facebook, Skype, instant messaging, all of these tools make it possible now to maintain long-distance relationships. You may have people yourself that you stay in close touch with using one of these . . . tools.

But let's look again at these people texting in a café. We call this "social connectivity," and it's true that you can connect instantly with someone thousands of miles away, but it is not clear what the quality of that connection is – whether it can truly be called an intimate friendship.

I'm not saying these social-networking tools are bad – and I think they can be vital to sustaining an existing friendship. But as far as making new friends – well, think about this verb that we use on Facebook – "friending" . . . "to friend" - just how meaningful is it to say "I have 683 friends on Facebook!" Are they really friends?

In conclusion, in terms of human history, social networking is a relatively recent phenomenon, so . . . we do not know what impact it will have on the nature of friendship. But I think it is safe to assume that friendship will survive. We are by nature social animals, we all want and need people in our lives that accept us and love us for who we are. The people we love – and who love us back – are our friends.

 Unit 4: Interpersonal Relationships
CD3 TR20 **Chapter 8: Love**

Getting Started: Listening for details, page 145

1.

Les: My name is Les. I'm a librarian. I'm divorced and in my late thirties. I enjoy listening to jazz and going to movies, museums, that kind of thing. I'm looking for someone who kinda likes the same things, I guess.

2.

Michael: My name is Michael. I'm a doctor, and I work very hard. I like to climb mountains in my spare time. I'm 35 years old, and I'd like to meet an attractive, younger woman.

3.

Alicia: My name is Alicia. I want to meet a kind, dependable man who will be a good father to my two children, who are four and six years old. I'm a computer engineer.

4.

Frank: My name's Frank. I'm a junior high school teacher. When I'm off in the summer, I love to garden and play baseball. I'm 37 years old.

5.

Sara: My name is Sara, and I'm an artist. I'm in my early forties. I guess I'm kind of shy, but I'd like to meet someone I can talk to about art and books, things like that.

6.

Suzanne: I'm Suzanne, and I'm, like, really into the healthy lifestyle. I'm in my mid-twenties, but I'm looking for a more mature man who makes good money and everything.

Interview Part 1: Courtship

CD3 TR21 **Listening for specific information,** page 147

Interviewer: Ann, how long have you and Jim . . . how long have you been married?

Ann: Thirty-three years, 33 years, right?

Jim: That's right!

Interviewer: Hmm. And that's a long time!

Ann: It is a long time.

Interviewer: Um, so I wanted to ask you, how did you initially get interested in each other?

Jim: We met when, uh, I was a senior in college and Ann, uh, was a senior in high school. And she lived in a small town about seven miles from where I was studying, and I was attending the same little country church where she and her family went, and that's how we met.

Ann: Uh-huh.

Interviewer: So, Ann, you were a high school senior.

Ann: That's right – I was sixteen.

Interviewer: Here was this older man!

Ann: I was 16 years old and I just thought he was the best person I'd ever met in my life. I just fell head-over-heels in love with him immediately at age 16. But at age 16, you usually fall head-over-heels in love with a lot of people. But this one stuck, and I had to wait 11 years before he actually proposed and we got married, which is kind of a long time.

Interviewer: Yeah!

Ann: But at age 16, I certainly wasn't ready to get married anyway. My, one of my greatest fears after I met him and decided pretty much then and there that he was the man I wanted to marry – but my greatest fear was that he would marry my sister, who was three years older than I am and therefore more his age, and I was so relieved when my sister married someone else.

Interviewer: Now, did Jim give you any encouragement? I mean, 11 years, that's a long time to wait.

Ann: Verrrrry little.

Interviewer: Well, Jim, uh, were you as interested in Ann from the beginning as she was in you?

Jim: Yes, I was, but I wasn't very good at showing it, I think, sometimes. And I really, I really realized after I finished medical school and I was doing my internship out in Seattle –

Ann: Now this was 10 years after we met.

Jim: That I, there was a big hole in my life, and I realized what that hole was – that I didn't have, didn't have Ann with me, and so I came to New York while Ann was getting her master's degree at Columbia. She'd just come back from two years in the Peace Corps in Ethiopia. And, uh, I brought many pictures of Seattle to show her 'cuz I understood she was considering a job in Philadelphia – teaching – when she finished. So, I brought all these pictures of Seattle – what a beautiful place it is – and, to encourage her that this was where she should come and, uh –

Interviewer: A rather oblique proposal!

Jim: Kind of oblique. But then the next spring, I was visiting back in New York, and I got a call from this wonderful older lady in our church – Aunt Amy [*laugh*] was her name – or that's what everyone called her – and Aunt Amy called up and she said, "If you're really interested in that Ann, you'd better get yourself down here 'cuz she might go off and marry one of the Peace Corps people she worked with."

Ann: That's true.

Jim: Well, I got right in the car, and I drove 67 miles down to her home, and I asked her mother – her father had died some years before – and I asked her mother for permission to . . .

Ann: This is true!

Jim: . . . to have Ann's hand and, uh, she was very–

Ann: She was very happy!

Jim: Very pleased. And then I proposed to Ann.

Interviewer: And Ann was very happy!

Ann: Ann was very happy!

Jim: And I was very happy!

Interviewer: Yeah!

Ann: It was a long time coming, but it was very much worth the wait. But I realize that there were several times when I came very close to marrying someone else, and I, I feel very fortunate that I, that I –

Interviewer: Yeah! That you waited.

Ann: Yeah!

Now complete the steps in your book.

Interview Part 2: Making Marriage Work

CD3 TR22 **Listening for specific information,** page 147

Jim: I think one of, one of the really nice things about, uh, about our relationship and our, our marriage has been that from the very beginning it never was all me or all Ann. There were, there were so many things that we had both done. Whenever we went out, it'd be, "Well, tell me about the time you went looking for elephants in Ethiopia," and she would remember something that, to ask me to tell friends, and we were both proud of what each other had done, so it wasn't a one-sided kind of thing. And that's, that's been the way it's been through the 33 years, too. I think that both of us have been not only husband and wife but also best friends. And, uh, proud of each other.

Ann: Uh-huh! And we share a lot of, a lot of interests. I think that's one of, one of the things that's made our marriage very, very strong.

Interviewer: What interests, for example?

Ann: Well, classical music. We love going to concerts.

Jim: Cross-cultural living – learning the history and learning some of the language – and, uh, we've worked in places all over the world.

Ann: And we both love outdoors and gardening, walking. We both come from very strong, very loving families, and our families are very important to us. And, um, our faith is very important to us, our involvement in our church, uh, and just the way we see people and the way we like people to be treated, and caring for others and that kind of thing.

Interviewer: Uh-huh. Are there . . . in what way do you think you complement each other? I mean, do you have differences that work to your advantage?

Jim: Ann, uh, Ann does the financial management for our family. If I did, I think we'd both be in jail by now because I hate paying bills and keeping records, and Ann is very meticulous about it. She also has a phenomenal record of our 30 years together.

Interviewer: She's the historian?

Jim: And they're all catalogued neatly in albums where they can be seen, not stuck in drawers, which is what I would do, or a . . . And it's wonderful because friends will come from 10 years ago, and we'll pull out an album, and it'll have pictures that they remember. It's very meaningful. And that's a talent I don't have at all.

Ann: I think that there's several, there's several things that make our marriage very special, and I think strengthen almost any relationship. And one is – I think Jim has alluded to it before – respect for each other. We both respect what the other does, and we're committed to our marriage. And we give each other space when we need to have time alone, but then we love to be together! We just love to spend time being in each other's company. We enjoy each other. At least I enjoy being with you!

Jim: Definitely I enjoy being with you!

Interviewer: Yeah. Can you think of experiences over the years that have particularly bonded you?

Ann: Mmm . . . Oh, yes!

Jim: Working overseas –

Ann: Living in a tent for three months –

Jim: In the desert in Somalia.

Ann: That was a fairly bonding experience. And of course our two children have bonded us.

Jim: Oh yeah.

Interviewer: Now, did you, did you know before you got married how many kids you wanted to have?

Ann: We knew that we wanted to have children. We didn't talk numbers, except I remember somewhere thinking that maybe six would be nice.

Interviewer: Six!

Jim: I remember!

Ann: And then we thought maybe four, and then after we had two boys we decided that two was just fine. But that was a bonding experience – raising our two sons – going through being parents for them as young children, and the teenage years, which were not necessarily the happiest of times.

Jim: They were, uh, challenging.

Ann: And now our sons are old enough so that we treat each other as equals. All four of us are adults now, so when we get together, it's just a wonderful adult-to-adult relationship.

 Interview Part 2: Making Marriage Work

CD3 TR23 **Listening for digressions, page 149**

1.

Ann: I just fell head-over-heels in love with him immediately at age 16. But at age 16, you usually fall head-over-heels in love with a lot of people. But. this one stuck, and I had to wait 11 years before he actually proposed and we got married, which is kind of a long time. **But at age sixteen**, I certainly wasn't ready to get married anyway.

2.

Ann: . . . one of my greatest fears after I met him and [*short pause, then spoken more quickly*] decided pretty much then and there that he was the man I wanted to marry – but **my greatest fear** was that he would marry my sister, who was three years older than I am and therefore more his age, and I was so relieved when my sister married someone else.

3.

Jim: But then the next spring I was visiting back in New York, and I got a call from this wonderful older lady in our church – Aunt Amy was her name – or that's what everyone called her – and **Aunt Amy called up**, and she said, "If you're really interested in that Ann, you'd better get yourself down here 'cuz she might go off and marry one of the Peace Corps people she worked with."

4.

Jim: Well, I got right in the car and I drove 67 miles down to her home, and I asked her mother – her father had died some years before – **and I asked her mother** for permission to . . .

Ann: This is true!

Jim: . . . to have Ann's hand . . .

 In Your Own Voice: Showing interest, page 154

CD3 TR24 **Ann:** Thirty-three years, 33 years, right?

Jim: That's right!

Interviewer: Hmm. And that's a long time!

Ann: It is a long time.

Ann: and I had to wait eleven years before he actually proposed and we got married, which is kind of a long time.

Interviewer: Yeah!

Ann: . . . there were several times when I came very close to marrying someone else, and I, I feel very fortunate that I, that I –

Interviewer: Yeah! That you waited.

Ann: Yeah!

Ann: . . . we share a lot of, a lot of interests. I think that's one of, one of the things that's made our marriage very, very strong.

Interviewer: What interests, for example?

Ann: Well, classical music. We love going to concerts.

Ann: We knew that we wanted to have children. We didn't talk numbers, except I remember somewhere thinking that maybe six would be nice.

Interviewer: Six!

Jim: I remember!

 Lecture: Dr. Robert Atkins, "Love: What's It All **About?"**

CD3 TR25 **Before the Lecture: Taking advantage of rhetorical questions,** page 156

1. Why do you fall in love with one person but not another person?
2. A lotta people might like a ten, but if you're a five, then who are you gonna end up gettin' married to?
3. If she graduated from graduate school, and he flunked outta kindergarten, do you think that relationship is gonna last very long?
4. Same age or about. Now, what's kinda the accepted age range?
5. Now, what about the idea that opposites attract?
6. You know that story of Romeo and Juliet?

 Taking advantage of rhetorical questions, page 156

CD3 TR26 1. Why do you fall in love with one person but not another person? Well, the sociobiology people, they would tend to say that you fall in love unconsciously, with somebody that's a good genetic match. Or somethin' like that
2. A lotta people might like a ten, but if you're a five, then who are you gonna end up getting married to? Well, probably somebody closer to a five
3. If she graduated from graduate school, and he flunked outta kindergarten, do you think that relationship is gonna last very long? Probably not.
4. Same age or about. Now, what's kinda the accepted age range? Usually five to ten years, with exceptions, of course.
5. Now, what about the idea that opposites attract? And you've probably heard that, that's kinda the complementary theory, or complementarity.
6. You know that story of Romeo and Juliet? You know, their families hated each other, and they said, "You stay away from him!" "You stay away from her!"

Lecture Part 1: "The Matching Hypothesis"

Outlining practice, page 158

CD3
TR27

This seems to be one of the more difficult topics to discuss. What is this thing called love? It seems everybody has a different idea about love. Why do you fall in love with one person but not another person? Well, the sociobiology people, they would tend to say that you fall in love unconsciously, with somebody that's a good genetic match. Or something like that. "Boy, she'd produce nice kids, so I love her!" Now, sometimes, women like guys that are tall, and muscular. Well, the sociobiologist would say that, well, they would produce a good, you know, gene pool. You know, that's why we like tall muscular types – or something like that. Now, even though you might like somebody – and you say, "Wow, she's beautiful – she's definitely a ten!" – you know, a lotta people might like a ten, but if you're a five, then who are you gonna end up getting married to? Well, probably somebody closer to a five. We tend to marry people like that, people that're like we are. We tend to really like people that're like we are. And that's homogeneity, or similarity. Some people call this the matching hypothesis – that we tend to be attracted to somebody that's like us. In fact, you're apt to stay married, too, if you married somebody that's like you are.

Of course, the matching part is more than just the physical. Maybe you've seen a couple walking down the street and said, "Wow, what is she doing with him?" Maybe she's a ten and he's a three, or something, or the other way around. And what that is, that's when you match up with someone, first, you notice the physical package, but then you start adding things in, like their personality, their job, their intelligence, and maybe when you look at the total, you might decide that they're a good match for you even if physically maybe they're not.

What else? Like, let's see, what'd be some things that . . . ? One would be the same educational background. If she graduated from graduate school, and he flunked outta kindergarten, do you think that relationship is gonna last very long? Probably not. Like, for example, I recall one student in a four-year college – a long time ago – that she didn't go on to graduate school because she was afraid it would break up the marriage. And he'd only graduated from high school. She's graduated from college. And he kept bugging her about being a college graduate. "You're so smart! Why don't you do it!" Right? "Well, you're the college-educated one!" Y'know, that sorta thing. So, she didn't wanna have even more of a gap, so she actually stayed down, and you might say, 'cuz he didn't wanna go up. Now that's kinda too bad. So, we tend to marry somebody similar in education. Often you met 'em in school. What else should they be the same about? Uh, interests! You'd have about the same interests often. So, what else? Maybe the same values? OK. Same religion, maybe. Same race. Same age or about. Now, what's kinda the accepted age range? Usually five to ten years, with exceptions, of course. But usually within five to ten years. What else would there be? Socioeconomic status, age, education, race, religion, values, interests, things like that.

Lecture Part 2: "The Matching Hypothesis (Continued) and Other Theories"

Outlining practice, page 159

CD3
TR28

OK, so, generally the more similar you . . . are, the more apt you are to stay married. And that really works. But you might say, "Well, gee, Bob! I'm a guy who flunked kindergarten, and my wife has a graduate degree." Or, "My mom has a degree, and my dad never graduated high school." Or what? I dunno. "He's Catholic and she's Jewish," or "She's 23 and he's 42," or whatever it might be. And, "Hey, they've been doin' fine!" That could be. But, as a general rule, the more different you are in these, it just increases your probability of getting a divorce. We also tend to find people who have similar politics to what we have. If you're liberal, you'll tend to marry someone that's liberal. Or a conservative will marry a conservative 'cuz you don't wanna marry someone that keeps telling you you're wrong. So, we also marry someone who sorta validates our ideas. We're kinda psychologically comfortable with those people. And, as I said, these marriages have a greater chance of lasting.

Now, what about the idea that opposites attract? And you've probably heard that, that kinda the complementary theory, or complementarity. I dunno why it is academics try to make big words outta little words. Instead of the difference theory, y'know, they say the complementary theory or complementarity, or something like that. But anyway. Difference. Well, that can work for magnets. With people, difference is not, it doesn't work as well as similarity does, but it can be a factor. Like if one person is dominant, are they better off with another dominant person, or are they better off with a person that's more submissive, that likes people telling 'em what to do? Probably a dominant person is more apt to marry a submissive person. And maybe he or she likes the other person to be dominant and that works out OK. So, there is something to that. Probably two dominants don't work well, or maybe two submissives don't work well: "Whaddayou wanna do?" "I dunno, whatever. Whadda you wanna do?" "I dunno. Whatever." So, maybe, so probably won't work too well. But, in general, the research that we have says that people that marry someone that's like they are tend to stay together.

One other factor that can bring a couple together is called the "Romeo and Juliet effect." You know that story of Romeo and Juliet? You know, their families hated each other, and they said, "You stay away from him!" "You stay away from her!" So, what did Romeo and Juliet do? Yeah, they got married. So, the Romeo and Juliet theory says the more opposition you face to a relationship, from parents or friends, or whoever, the more attractive that relationship is to you. The more people say, "Don't! You shouldn't!" the more you wanna do it. Pretty interesting, huh? And it turns out these couples usually stay together, too.

So, those are some of the things that bring people together. And probably the most important thing to remember is the similarity idea – that we tend to be attracted to and happy with people who are like us.